An Artist's Guide to
Living by Your Brush Alone

An Artist's Guide to

Living by Your Brush Alone

by Edna Wagner Piersol

Chapter Illustrations by
Howard Munce

North Light Publishers

Published by North Light, an imprint of
Writer's Digest Books, 9933 Alliance Road,
Cincinnati, Ohio 45242.

Manufactured in U.S.A.
First Printing 1983

Library of Congress Cataloging in Publication Data

Piersol, Edna Wagner.
   Living by your brush alone.

   1. Art—Vocational guidance. I. Title.
N8350.P53   1983   706'.8   83-15123
ISBN 0-89134-063-7

Book designed by Noel Martin.

Dedicated to Ila Davis,
Who Left My Life Too Soon
and to All My Dear Friends,
in Whose Hearts
Is My Only Real Home

Contents

Introduction

It is easy to become a starving artist. It comes naturally – no special skills required. But learning how to survive supported only by your paint brush, while remaining true to your own ideals of art – that is another thing. Don't think it will ruin you as an artist to make money by working at it. More likely, the process will improve your approach to life and, in turn, will make you a better artist.

Take a look at the Old Masters. What did they have to do to survive as artists? Was Michelangelo allowed to be himself? Not really. He was trained in Ghirlandaio's workshop and Bertoldo's school in the Medici gardens. No doubt, he had to abandon work he wanted to do in order to meet the demands of the day. Yet he was so independent in his assigned tasks that his talent came through as strongly as if he had been allowed to follow his own dictates.

There are many books these days telling us how to paint, but what about how to *live* as artists? How do we survive in the real world and remain free to paint and create?

One way is to realize that we *can* do it. We can find ways to make a living as artists in a freer way than was open even to artists like Michelangelo. Usually we can live exactly as we want without sacrificing our standards. So don't throw up your hands sighing, My God, she wants me to worry about selling my work. I don't care if you ever sell. But don't complain if you then have to trudge through life, working at a job you don't like when you could be living, happily, by your brush alone . . . creating pictures every day of your joyous life.

Chapter One

Courage to Live by Your Brush Alone

Standing before a group of artists, lecturing on the merits of self-assurance, I watched the facial expressions of those assembled in front of me. The looks flew back questioning: How did you have the courage to take off and begin to live by your brush alone? The truth is, I didn't. But I needed to live that way so strongly that courage didn't figure in my thinking. Experience taught me many things – things that can benefit every artist. When you are trying to live on your own, your worst enemy is yourself.

We tend to put ourselves into categories. What we say we are, we become. If we call ourselves unsuccessful artists, that's what we will be. When we say we can't do something, we usually mean we are afraid to try. There is one sure way to never fail: never try.

I have learned to ignore fear. I've told myself I am a successful artist because I am a good artist. Try it. If you want to live by your brush alone, it is possible.

What do you think would happen if you stopped someone on the street and asked if he'd like to own a fine painting? I doubt that anyone would say no. Few other products garner a more positive response. Your only problem is to get a painting to each person who wants one at a price he can afford – and a price that will also earn you a little profit.

Choosing Your League

It was nearly two years after I began living solely from my painting that I finally began to believe I was *doing* it. It was too good to be true – living the way I wanted without fear of tomorrow. Although I joke about it, a starving artist I am not. How did this come about? It started when I realized that *I am the one who chooses the league in which I want to play.*

If I had decided to be a "nobody" all my life, I would probably have been successful at it. But I wanted to *be* successful and I set my sights on my goal. I decided what kind of clothes I wanted to wear and what hobbies I liked, and I set out to make it all come true.

What do you want to do? Would you like to sell thousands of dollars worth of paintings a year in outdoor shows or do you want to become the next Picasso? It's all up to you. Don't try to hide behind some imagined limitation, such as "that's the only type of thing I can do." You are the one who decides where you will be successful. No one is going to tell you to step to the front of the line . . . everyone is too busy trying to get there themselves. It's easy to play the role of the "misunderstood" artist. Poor you; no one likes your work; no one ever appreciates you. Baloney!

What you have to do is tell the world and yourself that you *are* worth something. It's amazing how people respond to positive thinking. When articles were first written about me, I was astounded at how people believed what was written just because it appeared in print. I had won a number of awards, but nobody took much notice until an article appeared in the *Pittsburgh Post Gazette*. Then even my friends began to believe I was an artist. Didn't they realize I had told the reporter everything he wrote? I could have said anything – but I didn't. It's better to stick to the truth, but record all of your accomplishments in their best light.

The world appreciates those who appreciate themselves. If you don't like what you are and what you are doing, then *change*. You can do it – and it doesn't matter whether you are male or female. Being an artist is not a sex issue. Gender might pose a problem along the way if, for example, you are a mother or the sole provider for your family. But there are usually ways to deal with such problems. Deserting your brush will probably only compound your difficulties.

Full-time Art

Creating pictures must be the focal point of an artist's life. One of the most devastating ideas to stick in an artist's mind is that art cannot be pursued on a full-time basis. Nonsense! You don't have to waste your time doing something else to make a living.

As with any other profession, when you are well prepared, you can make a living at it. Your worst enemy is yourself. Don't limit your horizons or admit that you feel you can't do what you want to do. It takes work, *real* work, to be an artist. There is no time for making a living elsewhere. Being an artist is at least 90 percent hard work and maybe, if you are lucky, 10 percent talent. Once you realize that, you are on your way. Then you have two duties:

- To train yourself as well as possible; become as *good* as you can.
- To be true to yourself and *be* an artist. Work at it, and at *it*, only.

A certain amount of work will produce a certain amount of money. I'm constantly amazed at how consistent this principle is, and it's discussed in Chapter 3.

Why Copy Success? Be a Success

Artists talk a lot about influence and pull – politics in the art world. Does it exist? I suppose so, but I contend politics might get you in the spot in the art world where you want to be, but can never keep you out when you are good enough. What is "good"? Any artist who sincerely works to create pictures entirely his own is a "good" artist. As far as politics go, the best game to play is one of "kindness."

A successful artist friend of mine reminds me always that there is room for each of us in the world, that there is never any reason to compete with any other artist. If you are truly creating your own art, there is no competition. I've watched many potential artists become so fascinated with what makes others successful, and so busy trying to copy those successes, they forget to put the required effort into their own individuality. As a result, much potential is wasted because the effort is spent in the wrong direction.

In the process of trying to copy others' success, artists often fret about being accepted into professional groups. I hear colleagues bemoaning the fact that they were not accepted into this or that group or show. If such organizations are important for personal prestige, or useful as stepping stones to public recognition, there may be reason to seek membership. But, is it important to aspire to any outside "entity" when your real goal is to be an "entity" yourself? There are a lot of associations in the art world. I've helped to start some of them, so I'm not deriding them, but I wonder if Andrew Wyeth or Georgia O'Keefe ever had nagging worries about being accepted into any such group.

Most of the greats in art history had to start from nowhere, too. Read about them and see just how they went about it. Good reference books are readily available.

And Now to Courage

How do you find the courage to live by your brush alone? Courage is an elusive quality. It is rarely possessed, but it can be acquired. When I first set out on my own, I was terrified. I packed what I thought I needed in my little car, leaving the rest of my belongings in storage. This was a personal choice – I felt the need to travel right then. I began by peddling paintings around the country to make it possible to get where I wanted to go.

It turned out I took things I did not need. Some odd things, however, were necessary. Who needs a ceramic hand-thrown pot over one and a half feet high in a car? I did. That pot had been given to me by the Pittsburgh Watercolor Society after I'd served as president. I needed tokens of esteem and affection right then. They strengthened my courage.

It was a crazy two years before I settled down. Many times, I was tempted to quit and work for a regular paycheck, but I stuck to my goal. I told myself the minute I relied on anything but my painting to provide my living, I would be selling myself short. I am what I am – an artist. I live by my brush alone.

Chapter Two

Building Your Credentials

Credentials are your proofs of accomplishment, your credits. Build them by working hard to accomplish goals, then record the accomplishments.

Finding your own niche is the first step, because the type of credentials you need is governed by the kind of artist you want to be. If you haven't found your niche yet, Chapters 5 through 8 will help.

In building credentials, look for what will impress your chosen market. If you have decided to be an artist who makes his mark through galleries, don't waste time trying to land an illustration job with a magazine, even if the editor himself suggests it. There will always be well-meaning friends around with suggestions about what you should do. Artists seem particularly susceptible to this kind of flattery. Unless the suggestion fits your own plans, don't be tempted. It's so easy to be led down blind alleys. If a friend says you should illustrate a book (when you are in the middle of an abstract painting series) or suggests you start making your living by painting cats (just because you produced one good cat sketch), smile sweetly or punch him in the mouth – whichever suits your fancy – but don't listen. Follow your own lead to your own goals.

A certain amount of "dues" have to be paid, however, and they are a different cup of tea from the sidetracking ideas of friends. There are some tedious things you must fit into your plans. Don't try to skip the beginning stages of your career. For instance, if you have chosen fine art as your niche, you may have to spend time sitting in the local, outdoor shows before you move on to the galleries. If you choose to be a commercial artist, you may have to accept assignments you don't like before you can be selective. Keep samples of your jobs; and keep records of sales or awards in outdoor shows.

Determining Your Worth

A way of judging your own worth is needed next. Be sure you don't confine yourself to the beginning stage of your career after it's time to move on. How do you know how good you are and when it's time to move on? Be realistic. Find out what your clientele thinks. Most art directors and gallery directors are willing to talk to you about this. The hard part is listening. Don't take offense. If you want to make money as an artist, you have to please someone, somewhere. But take heart. What one gallery owner hates, another will love. Get several opinions and take what pleases you from all of their ideas. In other words, pick brains.

Get the opinions of the general art-buying public as well. Early in your career in fine art, outdoor shows are a great opportunity to discover a cross-section of people's likes and dislikes. People will tell you what they appreciate. Eavesdrop on their comments as they walk past and talk with them directly. They love to talk and you can educate them as they inform you. But, be careful. Don't allow yourself to be governed by what the public may want, but don't shut them out. Use only those ideas that fit into your own way of thinking. You will be surprised at what develops. When I choose popular subjects, I treat them my own way. I have won awards with paintings that have come out of a popular series on one subject, such as eagles. When you are immersed in the kind of painting you feel is interesting, when you are being totally creative, people become interested in what you are thinking. They will want your work because you did it. You touched them and opened a new avenue of thought for them. This is what art is all about.

When your work is selling well, it is time to raise prices. Sometimes, when it isn't selling, it is time to raise prices. People judge what they get by what they pay. Once, when things were slow, I doubled the price of my portraits and sold seven in one week.

Moving On

When you begin to feel confident in one arena, it's time to move on. Move up the ladder to whatever is next, in your judgment. If you feel it is time to exhibit in galleries, begin to interview them. Yes, you interview the gallery, but you don't have to let the gallery know you are doing so. Decide which gallery is right for you. Be pleasant about it. If a gallery director does not like your work, listen, and evaluate what he says about its quality. Nothing is gained by arguing with a gallery director, and you will make a valuable ally for the future if you make him feel he is your mentor and friend. If one gallery does not like your work, look for another. Look in another city, if necessary, until you find your own market.

Judge your worth by *your* accomplishments. Don't dwell on what you *haven't* done and don't judge your worth by what others think. If you judge your worth by others' opinions, you won't succeed. There are so many types of people in this world that you will always find conflicting opinions. Trying to heed them all is a sure way to constant confusion.

Work for those who like you for yourself. *Everyone* doesn't have to appreciate you; all you require is enough buyers to keep you working as an artist. When you become famous, everyone will *say* they appreciate you, but half of them won't know why.

My main criteria for a good piece of art is that it be truly creative, that it came from my own mind and is not imitative. Design and planning count, but most of all, good painting is not imitative.

Personality Plus

Building a *selling personality* along with your credentials is most important. Let's talk about how this can be accomplished.

It helps in selling your work and acquiring credits to be pleasant. Don't have a chip on your shoulder. Some artists like to feel that the world is being unkind to them. I remember, with distaste, one artist, a young man whom I met at an outdoor show – one of the places where I "paid my dues." This young watercolorist was an annual exhibitor. The first year I met him, our booths were side by side. I was amazed to observe him turn his back on many potential customers because they'd ask questions he felt were beneath his dignity. Still, he and I had a fairly good rapport. We manned each other's booths at coffee breaks and had some good discussions on art, but I was annoyed at his "anti-establishment" attitude. Art is so flexible and innovative that no one can ever really find the "establishment." Any artist who is worrying about it is fighting a ghost that he need not even conjure. Despite all this, I found the young man interesting and his work pleasing.

Two years went by before I saw him again. When we met this time, he had his hands full of display racks, but no paintings by which I could identify him. We greeted each other warmly. Unfortunately, he looked a lot like a photographer whom I had met at the same show two years earlier. I mistakenly asked how his photography was going. He bristled and glared at me and said, "Well, it's clear you don't remember my work, but I remember yours well and I *did* like it." (My work was sitting on the sidewalk right in front of me.) He turned on his heel and walked away, never speaking to me again during that show even though I tried to explain. I had liked his work, too. Should I be condemned because his face looked like someone else's? Nor was I the only victim of such petulant behavior. I saw him do the same thing to customers.

This kind of attitude is one we should fight constantly. Nobody *deserves* respect; one *earns* it. I fight my ego, and boost it at the same time, by helping people remember me. I say something like, "Well, hi! Good to see you again. Remember me? I'm the crazy lady who paints on tissue paper." All this is said before they can be embarrassed if they fail to instantly recall who I am. Make it a habit to think of others first. This may sound Pollyanna-ish but it works – even when you become a noted artist. How much nicer to be remembered as that famous artist who bothered to worry if someone remembered him, than to be thought of as that egotist who believed he should be remembered just because he thought he was famous. Building a personality that sells you as an artist actually builds your credentials, because the more you sell yourself, the more opportunities for accomplishment you create. So smile, and be pleasant. It pays big dividends.

Recording Accomplishments

As soon as you begin to achieve, start keeping a good record of your accomplishments and copies of any publicity connected with your shows and sales. Get a filing cabinet. Keep letters between you and clients plus letters of recommendation. Save the award certificates from shows, records and programs from your one-person shows when they come along, gallery requests – anything that shows the progress of your career. These papers actually are your credentials. Start a *record sheet* listing all of these accomplishments and organize them so that you can use the information profitably. When you are commissioned to do a painting, win any recognition or make a sale in a show, put that on your record sheet so you won't forget it. Yes, you will forget even important accomplishments as your work grows. Record any job, any small honor, any news clipping about you, no matter how small. This sheet is only for you to see and to keep your own record straight. You will use excerpts from it to prepare your finished *résumé*, the written record of your credentials. A résumé is what you hand to potential clients to give them a picture of your experience. Preparing your résumé is discussed in depth in Chapter 4.

To prove the value of well-kept records: One of the first things put on my private info sheet came back to haunt me in a pleasant way and it might have been easily forgotten if not recorded. This is how it went. When I was about fourteen years old, I painted a watercolor of a string of perch I had caught. I mixed my paint with water from the lake in which the fish had been caught. The watercolor painting won the top award in the Grange Fair Art Exhibit in the adult competition, which was fabulous to me at that age. Who would think that childish award still useful? It was. Just five years ago, a long time from my early award, a newspaper writer was doing an article on a show in which I had a watercolor of an abstract fish. I mentioned the earlier award to him. Immediately the feature of his article became a photo of me and my painting with the show director looking over my shoulder. The whole article was improved because no photo had been scheduled until the appealing "gimmick" presented itself.

Keep *clippings* on file along with your résumé information. Put everything that is ever printed about you in folders in chronological order. Keep a special cross-reference card file on them with subjects such as "fish" or "blue paintings" or "travel experience" in it. Many of your clippings will be useful in a number of categories.

Keep *color slides* of your paintings, made immediately after finishing each piece. Use these slides to enter shows (see Chapter 6) and for small, informal showings when you are making presentations of your work. Also have black and white glossy photographs, made by a professional, of all your best works. These will be invaluable when you get your presentations together.

Building Credits with Sales

How do you get the credits needed for a résumé? In other words, how do you find work? Go and look for it. Meet people. Being seen and heard are your biggest assets at the beginning. When you are seen, your work will also be seen. It is emotionally hard for artists to seek exposure of their work because producing art is so personal. We can't help feeling that a rejection of our work is a rejection of ourselves. Fight this attitude. Try to look at your sales approach as though you were selling apples instead of pictures. If you knock on someone's door and ask if they want to buy apples, they might tell you they want oranges, or they might say they had just bought apples. You wouldn't have a nervous breakdown over that, would you?

Try to make the selling fun. That way it won't be so hard on you. Learn to look at a potential buyer as someone whom you want to meet and enjoy rather than someone to be conquered. Try to fill the buyer's needs. Reach out.

Knock on doors. One day I was traveling through Georgia and I needed money. It was in the period of my life when I was searching to find myself after a divorce. Traveling on my own I was, literally, peddling paintings out of the back of my car. I had an appointment at an Atlanta office building. When I arrived, the office had a note on the door telling me the owner had to go out for half an hour and to please wait. Next door was an insurance agency with the word "Eagle" in its name. There was an eagle painting in my portfolio. I was in a good mood that day, although on the verge of starving. Maybe hunger had made me lightheaded, but it also gave me extra courage. Two pleasant young men were visible through the window and the office walls were bare.

I walked in and introduced myself, naming some of my credits in my introduction. I think I said something about being the artist lady who sold from the back of her car, that my most famous painting was of an eagle, and that it was in a museum collection. I told them their agency name demanded an eagle on the wall and that I had one in my car. The situation was bizarre enough to be fun for all and could be taken lightly, yet seriously at the same time. I was careful not to be too pushy, but before long they were asking to see the eagle. When I left, they had a new painting on their wall and I had enough money to travel on to Pennsylvania. I ate well that week and added a new credit to my name.

Seated Eagle, 24x20 inches, watercolor on tissue paper coated with wax, by Edna Wagner Piersol.

Several times eagle paintings like this one have saved my life and kept me eating. Not only have I sold them, but I have also traded a few for room and board.

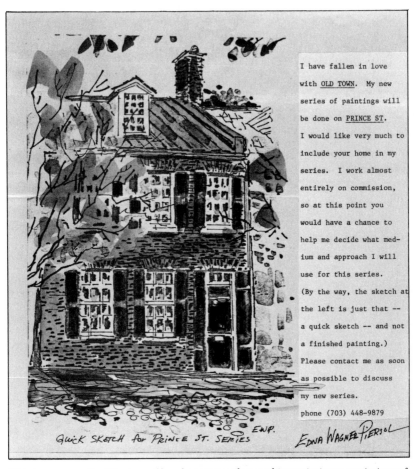

I have fallen in love with OLD TOWN. My new series of paintings will be done on PRINCE ST. I would like very much to include your home in my series. I work almost entirely on commission, so at this point you would have a chance to help me decide what medium and approach I will use for this series. (By the way, the sketch at the left is just that -- a quick sketch -- and not a finished painting.) Please contact me as soon as possible to discuss my new series.

phone (703) 448-9879

Quick Sketch for Prince St. Series   E.W.P.

Edna Wagner Piersol

This is an example of the type of brochure I use when seeking painting commissions of homes. It not only introduces me to the homeowners, but also gives them a hint of how charming their homes could look as paintings. The letter beside the drawing encourages them to contact me as soon as possible, and I make it easy for them by stating my phone number.

Another time, I had recently moved into a town that had a beautiful historic section. People bought, restored, and lived in these lovely old structures. I needed some new commissions. One day, while sightseeing, I was struck by a brainstorm. I got out my sketch pad and went to work. I sketched one or two houses, then I took photos. I went back to my studio and painted a small watercolor, using only grays so it

24

would reproduce easily. I had it reduced to a size that would fit on a nice little brochure and wrote a neat letter to be printed with it, informing those fifty homeowners that I was beginning a series of watercolors of each of their houses. I added my address and phone number, and waited. When commissions resulted, my credentials had grown.

"Looking for work" can be done in local art exhibits. You'll find art show listings in art magazines. Watch your local newspaper to find shows being held in your area. Often there are shows open to any artist. Enter your work exactly as described in the printed information that is always given out about an exhibit. Be careful to follow the directions to the letter. See Chapters 5 and 6 for more information on entering shows.

When the show is on the wall, be present and available. Meet everyone you can. If you are shy, make yourself talk to everyone who shows any interest in your work. They will be interested in you if you show an interest in them. I've even walked up to a person who was looking at my painting and said to them, "I wouldn't give you two cents for a Piersol painting." As they turn to me, their expressions are extremely interesting. By that time I'm laughing and introducing myself and we become friends. I don't know what I'll do the day someone says to me, "Neither would I." Oh, well, take the bitter with the better. If you keep forcing yourself to meet people, someone will want more artwork and you'll be there at the right time.

Creating Your Own Publicity

Another way to find work with your brush early in your career is to be open to doing some charity work for the publicity it offers. *Getting publicity* in order to find work is a big goal when you begin to live solely by your art. Artists are notorious for being impractical. Sometimes we don't realize that we can be "super-talented" and still be undiscovered. It is important for an artist to sell himself. If the first order of business is to become a good artist, then the second is to start to publicize yourself. Build your credentials, then see that they pay off.

Good public relations will not make up for weak art, but good art without good PR will go nowhere. Promotion, or "image," is invaluable and cannot be replaced. Don't kid yourself and think artists become well known because of "merit." Success almost never depends on merit alone.

When "seeking publicity" be sure it is handled subtly. Don't be pushy or obvious. People should not realize that publicity is what is being sought. Try to to find ways to make yourself interesting and newsworthy. Here is where your résumé record does its work. Go over it regularly and see what might best be exploited.

Clubs and church groups are always looking for ways to make money. Give them a free lecture demonstration which they can open to the public and get newspaper coverage. When you do a lecture or demonstration, you might get a commission from someone. If you aren't a public speaker, arrange a painting raffle. To live by your brush alone, a lot of time must be spent doing things that do not pay off immediately. Look for ways of getting around this fact of life. Try getting a club member to purchase your raffle painting at a nominal fee to cover your expenses. Get as realistic a price as you can. Perhaps your benefactor will pay close to your original asking price. He can then give the painting to the club to raffle off. This allows the buyer to deduct the painting from his taxes, the club to make money, and you to have your expenses paid.

There will be other times when it may enhance your reputation to give the painting outright. But watch this procedure – it may start a snowball rolling that you don't want. Your object, always, is to make your work pay your living expenses. Don't lose sight of that goal. It is a goal different from the one of being a good artist. They are two separate categories. If you have not convinced a club member, or the club itself, to purchase a painting in advance, try another approach. Be persistent in your trials to sell. Go one step beyond your feelings of propriety. This is hard to do, and worse if you're a little shy. I've found one pleasant way to be persistent is to single out someone in whom you have sensed a spark of interest, and simply tell that person, in private, that you would really like one of your paintings to go into his collection. Potential buyers find such an approach hard to resist. I always follow up any kind of interest with one phone call. I'm never obtrusive, just interested in having a new collector involved in my work and owning it.

Aim for one good publicity accomplishment per month. You can do your own publicity when none other is available, or until you build up enough confidence to try for splashy things like news articles. Remember my historic home series? In Chapter 4, I give specific directions on preparing promotional pieces, because to increase your publicity, you will need to have some kind of general mailing and handout pieces to give to prospective buyers. Get good help on this and pay for it.

I have a brochure on my workshops that was laid out by a designer who traded his work for one of my paintings. The brochure contains good black and white photos of five of my most accepted paintings, a photo of me, and a description of the five kinds of workshops I present to art groups. I have another card with a good reproduction (in black and white because of the expense involved in color printing) of one of my most appealing portraits. I hand out these leaflets to two very different kinds of clients: the portrait cards to people interested in fine art portraits and the workshop brochures to prospective students. I also mail these out, and that is what I am suggesting to you.

Do a good mailing once in a while. Clubs usually get their programs for the following year set up months ahead of time. I've found that a mailing around the middle of January (when people are just pulling out of the post-holiday doldrums) gets the most attention. Other good mailing months for promotion pieces are September and October – to seek commissions from clients thinking ahead to Christmas. You may become so busy that you have to create a waiting list for next Christmas, but mail when you get *their* attention, not for your convenience.

If you are a commercial artist, you *must* keep your name constantly before art directors without being too obtrusive. A neat card sent to art directors you already know, with a reproduction of your work and a note on the back, accomplishes this. Hand-written notes, even quickies on the margins of printed pieces, do wonders. The personal touch is the icing on the cake. It makes the receiver, no matter how important, feel *more* important.

Building your credentials is your most important "early career" or "starting over" task. So start by working hard; then keep a complete record of your accomplishments. You never know what will pay off. Get the record out before the public. Be ready when opportunity knocks to give information about yourself. It's hard to be egotistical, but try it – you might like it. Brag a little, but do it gently. Nobody loves a bore. Try my three A's for *accreditation:* accomplish – account – assert. First: Accomplish the work. Second: Keep a detailed account of what you have done. Last, but by no means least: Assert that you have done some great work.

Chapter Three

Strategy and Discipline

Exactly how much money do you need to make a living? How will you get it?

How many paintings, sold at your highest price, would produce your living expenses? How many would it take at your lowest price? Do you have enough markets to produce that income? How can you go about getting the markets you need? Where have the bulk of your sales been made? How can you exploit that market even more? Expand to other cities? Advertise more? Make personal contacts? These are questions to ask when planning strategy and making a plan of attack.

Maybe you need to raise your prices. Never lower a price, always raise it. There are psychological prices. People who will pay $125 for a painting, will not pay $100. $1,000 is a bad price; $1,500 is good. I don't know why psychological prices exist. Perhaps the subconscious of the buyer tells him that if an artist wants $100 for a painting, it is an arbitrary figure; but if the artist wants $125, the price has been figured out by an evaluation of cost.

If a potential buyer notices that a price has gone up, he may assume that the overall value of the artist's work has gone up.

Let's say you want to make $20,000 per year. Don't let fear seize you; it can be done. If your paintings are selling for $150, that means you have to produce 133.33 paintings per year to produce $20,000. Let's make it easier on ourselves and say you will produce 135 paintings per year. But you haven't allowed any money for expenses yet. I find that about one-third of the selling price of the paintings drains off in expenses, so that means you will have to produce an extra forty-five paintings to cover expenses. This brings the total to 180 paintings a year. Don't panic. That is one painting every 2.2 days. If you are like me, when you are really rolling, you can start three to five paintings in a day. Painting that much forces you to grow as an artist.

Don't forget, we are selling your paintings at a very low price. You may have to do that for a while. Your price will soon go up. When you reach the $2,000 per painting level, you will have to produce less than 1.3 paintings per month to make ends meet. You say you are not ready for $2,000 painting sales yet? Let's try our breakdown with $350 paintings. That only requires you to produce a painting every 4.05 days. Not bad at all. Not even two a week – and your price *will* go up. One portrait per month and one other commission keeps me in the income bracket in which I choose to live. There are a lot of advantages for an artist who keeps a living style way above income level. Let's go on with our plan of attack and see how it all works out.

It's hard for an artist to think in terms of producing half a painting a day or producing one painting every other day. It is much better to carve out large blocks of work. For instance, schedule a show of sixty paintings. That's one third of your year's work at the low $150 per painting rate. Work toward that end and plan how you are going to sell those paintings.

Self-Discipline

There are two categories into which your work falls. First comes production. Then comes selling. It would be nice to neatly tie up each group and deal with it separately, but that doesn't work. You must deal with these categories simultaneously.

You must be disciplined in both production and selling. Self-discipline is the key to success. Work a certain number of hours and the same number of hours each day. Don't say you aren't always inspired. Any artist who waits to be inspired is likely to be a starving artist. I'm inspired to eat three times a day, so my brush has to be inspired to move at least three times a day. The best inspiration is picking up the brush. When you feel you do not have an idea in your head, let your technical knowledge take over. You'll find you produce a better painting when your mind is not racing ahead of the brush, tripping over itself, and getting your hands all tangled up in the mess.

Some of you work a nine-to-five job. Discipline will still get you enough time to become a successful artist, but remember, working at anything that takes you away from art defeats your goal. I'm only mentioning other jobs here to show you that discipline will solve any problem – even the problem of a mundane job. I'm hoping that if you do work from nine to five, your job is art-related. In that case, my wrath does not reach you in the same intensity as it would if your job is outside the art field.

If you find five hours a day at least four days a week to work at painting, you can still graduate to living by your brush alone. What would happen, though, if you gave yourself a real chance by borrowing enough money to live on for a year? Borrow against your house or your good looks, whatever you've got, and set out to live the way you want to. Are you one of those who stays tied to an unhappy job just because you have built up some retirement or you have hospitalization? Believe it, you can get those same things for yourself (see Chapter 9).

Organizing Work Hours

Your first discipline is to set up work hours for yourself – a minimum of five hours a day. Sometimes it does not seem that you are working when you are. I spend a lot of hours each week thinking, writing notes, making scribbles (fascinating small designs done with my eyes closed, described later), and humming to myself. A writer friend of mine observed that I worked about two full days per week in order to keep my larder full. But he didn't count all the humming and scribbling, so he misjudged me terribly.

You can't be painting every minute that you are working. A lot of time must be spent doing things, from humming and scribbling to matting, framing, delivering to framers, picking up supplies, writing publicity releases, and keeping records. You don't hold a brush nearly as much as you'd like. But it all must be done. Some days you will paint many more hours than others. I didn't say you can't work eight or ten hours per day or even more; just that you must clear five hours for work each day or you won't succeed.

I know a young woman who gets up at five and has two full hours of painting in before anyone else gets up. She takes a nap with her baby in the afternoon, then puts in another three hours from seven to ten while her husband babysits. Another friend of mine, now one of the most famous watercolor artists in the country, owned a commercial studio. He always put in a full day there only to come home and work four or five hours, four nights per week. He sold his studio recently and "retired" to full-time painting and teaching. It's just a matter of organizing. Face that, get at it, and don't be discouraged until you get the hang of it.

Weekly Schedules

Spend time whipping yourself into shape. Develop and write down a schedule. Stick to it religiously. If it does not work, revise it. Revise it *only* if it really doesn't work, not because of laziness or discouragement. There is something that I fight which may be your enemy, too: procrastination. It seems I'll do anything in the world to put off painting, the one thing I love most. I think that no matter how much we love that brush, we also hate it. It forces us to prove ourselves each time we pick it up. When it is time to start to paint, I can always think of ten letters that need answering, two phone calls that must be made – I really must go out to get some masking tape. This is one more reason that it is imperative to stick to your schedule.

Often it is easier to plan by the week rather than trying to set up a rigid, daily schedule. I use about fifteen hours per week in pure painting and sketching. The rest of my work time is scheduled around the painting like this:

Monday	*Morning:* Answer mail. Paint.
	Afternoon: Mount or frame paintings.
Tuesday	*Early Morning:* Paint.
	Late Morning: Keep business appointments, if necessary.
	Afternoon: Appointments or painting.
Wednesday	*Morning:* Paint
	Afternoon: Do errands, pick up supplies, take work to printers, deliver paintings, etc.
Thursday	*Morning:* Answer mail. Appointments or mounting and framing paintings.
	Afternoon: Appointments or record keeping.

	Evening: Teach painting class.
Friday	Paint all day.
Saturday	Sketching trips; art group activity.
Sunday	Enjoy life a lot. Spend some time in the evening organizing the next week's work.

These hours must be juggled at times to make allowances for appointments at other people's convenience. When this happens, keep a record of how many painting hours you have sacrificed. Make those hours up within the week. Two mornings a week, from eight to nine, I answer letters. Many days I work overtime but never "undertime." Some business calls can be made in the evenings; some evenings I mount or frame paintings, etc.

Tuesday, Wednesday and Thursday are the best days to schedule the kind of work where interaction with business people is required. Any salesman will tell you that those days are *the* selling days.

Don't ever forget this is your *job* and it requires the same dedication as any other kind of job. We artists work for ourselves, and the boss – me – is a stickler for getting things accomplished. I've got to tell you, though, my boss rewards me generously. No other boss in this world would give me *all* the profit.

I can't stress enough the need for establishing a work schedule and sticking to it. When you first go into the studio on schedule, you may experience panic. "I have to work, I have to work, I *have* to work *now?*" may be your reaction. Relax. Spend the first hour or so humming and scribbling. Your ideas will fall into place. See what productive work humming can be!

Scheduled Solitude

Being alone and undistracted during the most creative periods of your work week is essential. You must find ways to impress your family and friends with this unalterable fact. That's hard to do. Writers have the same problem. We work at home so people think we don't work at all. Sometimes we even have trouble convincing *ourselves* that our time is not our own. We artists tend to be dreamers and discipline comes hard.

I think it's important to control the kind of people you let into your life. You don't need kibitzers who are time wasters. You must be hardhearted. People always want to know what an artist is doing. They think that because you work at home, you can be bothered at any time. Your retired friends and relatives may take to dropping into your studio for coffee. It will happen without you realizing it.

There have been times in my life when I didn't seem to be getting anything done and I didn't know why. Then I took a good look over the past week. One friend had wanted me to go to a museum with her and explain the latest show; another had wanted to take me shopping to select linens for her niece's wedding gift because I "knew color." If I had worked at a nine-to-five job as a decorator, she would never have presumed to ask; but worse, I, like a fool, had gone.

I love my friends. The hardest thing in the world is to say, "No, I'm sorry. I do not have time." Your friends can make or break your mood. That's why isolating your working time and your working space can't be stressed enough. You are often your worst enemy on this score, so take time at least once a month to evaluate your work hours and the kind of people with whom you are associating. Try to get the greatest number of people who will inspire you into your life, and those who don't inspire you, out. Hardhearted? Yes.

If you do not live alone, schedule your work time when no one else is at home. While I was raising my family, my production hours were nine to three. Sometimes, on days when I was painting, I didn't even eat lunch. My children were in school and that was my only time to work and work hard I did.

If you do not have a time when everyone else leaves the house, consider studio space away from the home or away from its center. You must remove yourself from all distractions. If someone so much as kindly offers you a cup of tea, it may shatter the mood. Some creative stress is good for you and it comes along even in the most secluded situation. Squirrels chatter. Boats pass on the river; a truck rumbles along the road. Just remove all the unwanted interruptions you can. For instance, the telephone: what a jarring shock in the middle of a brush stroke! You can control that evil ring with an answering service. You can't work without one. In my area, a good twenty-four-hour service, with a real person's voice on the end of it, costs about the same amount per month as I get for one good pen-and-ink sketch. You can afford that. Just sell one sketch a month that is earmarked to pay for the service.

There are mechanical answering devices that aren't as expensive as real people. I just happen to like a live voice because I live alone and hear my own voice enough. My schedule calls for me to turn on the answering service at nine and not pick up my calls until ten-thirty or eleven when I feel like a break. Then, if I absolutely have to return a call before noon, I do. Otherwise I pick up messages again at four and return all calls then. By that time I am so satisfied with getting so much work done that my assurance is sure to show in my voice. My service answers twenty-four hours a day, so if I go out sketching, to dinner, or away for several days, I won't miss any commission calls. Sometimes opportunity rings only once. The answering service is a must, and remembering to turn it on is also essential.

Home Studio Space

My arrangement for living and working is that I have combined everything into one apartment. I hide my studio equipment in the kitchen. During nonworking hours, my work table is covered with a floor-length cloth and looks like a comfortable, slightly oversized kitchen table. When the cloth is removed, a large cube on casters is revealed. One side of the cube is open, exposing shelves. Those shelves hold 30 x 40-inch illustration boards, paper, and other gear under the work table's ample top.

My other painting paraphernalia, like paint tubes and brushes, is stashed in a fishing kit and stored in the pantry. Over the years, this kit has been my constant companion. It holds everything and not only travels to my work table from the pantry, but also follows me all over the country in my car and has even ridden on horseback. It is my studio in a box.

I'm not one for being encumbered with a lot of possessions. I've never envied the artists with huge studios and gigantic equipment. If that's what you like, though, it can't hurt. I do like north light and I almost have it in my apartment, my light streaming in from north-northwest through the balcony window. The light has to travel through my dining room before reaching the kitchen, so I sometimes move my work into the dining area. The kitchen/studio is not overly large, so some other equipment is stored and used in a bedroom. There I have a huge walk-in closet where my photo equipment is stored; a slide projector sits in a table-bin on wheels. The table-bin came from a discount store and has two lower shelf-bins that hold slide trays, etc. I pull it out to use the projector on the white wall and wheel it to the

This is my work table in its disguise as a lovely dining table. Uncovered, the work table is exposed for what it really is: a movable work space and storage area. (Photos by Bob Young)

My gallery space tucked into a corner of my living room. (Photo by Bob Young)

kitchen when needed. (All my walls are a soft white so that they take projection and paintings equally well.) My file cabinet, large painting portfolios, an easel or two, and all other equipment needed for presentations to my clients are also stored in the big closet.

My gallery space is an L-shaped section of my living room. All furniture and visual distractions have been removed from that area. The walls hold about nine paintings at a time. Some hang while others rest on easels. So, for the price of an apartment, I have studio, gallery, and living space. Of course, I can't have an outdoor sign to denote the gallery, but my clients are drawn to me by other means of advertising and display described in Chapter 4. I have no trouble from neighbors about clients viewing my work and sitting for portraits. For all my neighbors know, I simply have a lot of friends. (Check the laws in your area regarding restrictions to operating a business in your home.)

If you don't live alone, you can still arrange your home to work for you. I have an artist friend who has a gorgeous house in a very lovely residential section. Her family has given over to gallery/studio space what would usually be the living room. Their large family room in the back of the house has become the living/family room. The front door leads directly into the studio. When her family leaves in the morning, my friend becomes the total artist. If she has an appointment in the evening, her family is in another world from the studio.

It's important to let the fact that you are an artist dominate your lifestyle. If you keep your studio back in a spare bedroom, it will be relegated to that status in your life. Your family will treat it as secondary to the rest of living. You will, too. What kind of impression do you make when you take a client to a bedroom to view paintings that you have to pull out from under the bed? When you are living by your brush, your style can't be "back bedroom."

Creative Ideas at Work

Getting ideas for work and deciding what you will work on becomes your next project. When you have an idea, go with it. Give it a good hard try. Don't fall into the trap of thinking that anyone can do what you are doing. Our creative minds are so high powered, we forget that others' brains don't work as ours do.

Even other creative brains seldom run along the same channel. Never stop doing something because you think that others could do it as well. I have instigated projects that I felt sure everyone else would know how to do. I thought I'd never get recognition for them. To my great delight, I was wrong. I did receive recognition and profit.

If an idea does begin to fail, get out fast! Reinvest your energy in another project right away and don't waste time crying over "spilt paint." It is good to have several painting projects going at one time, so that while one is incubating and another is beginning to fail, still another can be bubbling and keeping your spirits up.

Keep a running record of ideas that will produce income. Have a little notebook that you can keep with you. Write ideas in it for painting subjects and for promotions. A tape recorder is a good friend, too. Keep one with you and talk to yourself anytime. Good ideas are something you don't want to lose.

How long does it take to "drum up" business in an area? I find things begin to happen and money starts to come in after I have been working in an area for about a month. (The kinds of things you have to do to make this happen are covered in Chapters 2 and 4.) It takes time for your name to sink into buyers' minds. If you want to move to a new geographical area, don't be afraid to do it. What works in one area will work in another, but I recommend that you stay near a large urban area – stay accessible. The more people with available money, the more business for you. Look up the average income in an area or check at the area's chamber of commerce before you move. Right now, the area in which I live has a median income about 60 percent above that of the rest of the country. If you yearn to move to a mountain top, take into consideration how you will get to a market. If you can get to enough clients from your mountain, go to it. Otherwise, take the easier way out: Stay accessible.

Warm-Up Exercises

Your own working methods will evolve as you go, but I have used my plan of getting started each day for many years. Here is how it goes. Start at the same time each working day, as though you have a job in some place of business – as in truth you do. Each morning I get out of bed rather early, because I'm a slow starter. My work day does not begin until nine but I like to get up about six-thirty, so I can enjoy a leisurely cup of coffee, the view or the morning show on TV. This is also a time for communicating with my soul, for planning big things to come. Sometimes it's pure daydreaming, yet important and constructive. It's true that what you think you are, you will become. So, in the morning I spend some time enjoying the successful artist that I am. Then, when the hands of the clock reach 8:45, I have finished breakfast and am ready to get my mind in gear for creating. I don't start on a masterpiece right away. My favorite way of warming up is to do what I call blind squiggles.

Blind squiggles are designs done with eyes shut. First, take a sheet of typing paper and draw about six rectangles on it. Don't let the rectangles touch one another. Their size will be about 2 x 3 inches. You can control your hand better working in that size. Now, with your eyes open, place a ballpoint pen (the kind with a long barrel for easy handling) in an advantageous design spot inside one of the rectangles. This means you will not place your pen point in the exact center of the rectangle nor in the center of any of the quadrants of the rectangle. All of those spots are awkward for good designs. A good spot to place your pen is just a little to the right of the center of the rectangle and just below or above an imaginary line dividing the rectangle in half. Start here the first time. Now close your eyes and start to move your pen.

Make any kind of marks that you want, all the while keeping the size of the rectangle in mind with your eyes closed. Don't peek. Just make marks without lifting your pen from the paper. If you are in the mood for straight strong strokes, do them; if you prefer oval or rounded organic shapes, go with them. Continue to move your pen for several seconds so that you build up some marks, one over the other, keeping your eyes closed. Don't look at your squiggle creation yet.

Now, as you get ready to end this squiggle, do a few thrusts of the pen in a different direction or shape. All the time you are doing this, you should be thinking of the size and shape of your original rectangle. Now, as you open your eyes you'll be surprised to see what you have done. Keep these designs for future reference.

In your first one you may find you have gone out over the edges, or you made your design much smaller or larger than you thought. That's okay. Look at this design upside down, then sideways. What comes out? What could you turn it into? If you don't feel that the design is good, don't try to correct it. Do another. If you have gone out of the boundaries, try to stay more contained the next time. Concentrate harder on your rectangular space with your eyes closed. If you open your eyes while squiggling, you destroy the communication that you have set up with your subconscious.

40

An example of some of my blind squiggles, a creative way to start productive painting time and to have designs for the future.

Do one design after the other and analyze later. It is important to analyze only the marks inside the rectangle. Keep a bottle of typewriter correction fluid at hand to "white out" all the marks that extend over the borders. Look at the designs at all angles – upside down, sideways – to see which way each design works best.

Save all these squiggles. When you don't know what to paint or you need some inspiration on work you have been assigned, bring out a bunch of your "squiggles" and let your imagination wander over them. One will spark your imagination for a new approach to whatever kind of painting you must do that day. Your squiggles serve several purposes. They keep you in a running conversation with yourself; they provide designs for future paintings; they help you get started into a productive painting day – get your mind and hands working together; and they tell you much about your mood and what you need to conquer in your design thinking. Good paintings can grow from these squiggles.

As soon as I have put in one half-hour or so at squiggles, I go on to put in a full morning of painting. The squiggles have warmed me up, and I'm off – my hands, head, and heart all working in unison. I save today's squiggles for future use and get on to the work at hand.

My rule for beginning a painting is to find a squiggle and a design plan, then to follow a good definition of a painting. This is my favorite definition: A painting is an arrangement of areas of color, within another given area, so as to produce a desired effect. That's so easy it's hard!

Knowing When to Stop

When it comes to ending the painting, we all need some help. Artists have a joke about what it takes to produce a good painting: One artist to paint it and one to say stop. You can be your own backup artist if you follow some simple rules. First, stop working on the painting as soon as you give out the slightest sigh of boredom, or as soon as you don't know what to do next. Put the painting away for awhile . . . an hour or a day. After that, decide how to finish it by asking yourself four questions:

- Does the painting check out by the "four quarter method"?
- Does the painting have a warm or a cool dominance?
- Does the painting contain three values: light, medium, and dark?
- Where does the lightest light meet the darkest dark?

Let's take each question and consider it thoroughly.

First: the four quarter method. Tape your painting up on the wall. Stand back about ten feet, or as far away as is comfortable for viewing. Take two index cards (one in each hand) and hold them up at arm's length. Allow the lower left corner of the right card to barely touch the upper right corner of the left card. Close one eye so that you see two separate quarters of the painting. Concentrate on one quadrant at a time. Now, simply decide if that quarter "looks good." Is it exciting? Is it boring? If it's boring you will know it and you will know it's bad. After you have concentrated on one quarter, do the same with the other. Then reverse the cards and repeat the process until you have analyzed all four quarters. To find out what "good quadrants" should look like, go to a museum and look at famous paintings. Especially look at the works of the Old Masters. See how exciting different sections of many of the pictures appear. If you can't get to museums, use reproductions of famous paintings in books.

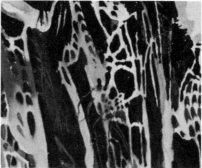

Looking at a painting using the four quarter method. Study one quadrant at a time. This painting, Earth Cellar by Barbara Gresham, is presented in its entirety in Chapter 10.

Second: warm or cool dominance in a painting. You have to be an accomplished artist to make a painting work with one half cool color and one half warm color. It's much easier to quickly add a little warm or cool to tip the scales in one direction or the other. Usually, this will pull the painting together effectively. Such dominance, although slight, does much to create a feeling of unity.

The third question is probably the simplest to see and the hardest to control. If your painting is weak in contrasting values, it will lack impact. That may be the effect you want. If so, okay. But, often a careful analysis shows that a clear definition of three distinct values is what the composition needs for unity and structure. Once again, tape the painting to the wall and stand back, Squint your eyes until they are barely open and you will see the painting in simplified value. If you feel you can't divorce your thinking from the painting's subject matter, turn the painting upside down – a good thing to do while answering all of the previous questions.

The fourth question to answer is where do your darkest darks touch your lightest lights? Where they touch will produce a strong visual attraction, a center of interest. Be sure this is the area you want the viewer to concentrate on. If these areas are in the wrong places, it is often easy to make adjustments by reducing some light colors. By altering the value in a white area, you can diminish its importance. For example, if the light area is on a white house, the house can be painted light blue or gray, or given a tint of any color, because white reflects all colors. Many artists have a fondness for making the sky a light value in landscapes. Often this creates an area of strong light against dark all along the horizon, tree or roof line, or whatever. The eye is drawn there, trapped in an unimportant path along that portion of the painting. I've found a medium value has definite advantages for skies. See what happens to the dynamism of your landscape with a darker sky.

When you have answered these four questions to your satisfaction, you have finished a painting with assurance. Never again will you need to wonder if a painting is done.

Painting Commissions

Make commission work reward your soul as well as your pocketbook. How do you do that? We all hate to do what someone else tells us to do. Most of us are a cantankerous lot. We can't help it. We have highly individual personalities. The trick to making commission work rewarding is to look for something in your client's thoughts that interests you. If he wants you to do a painting of his favorite cow, how can you become interested? Well, what does interest you? Color? Then become fascinated by how you can produce interesting colors on that cow. Design? What kind of squiggles have you produced that can be applied to the animal? Your client doesn't care *where* you place the cow, just so it looks like *his* cow. He will be impressed when you create a dynamic design.

I repeat my favorite definition of a painting usually attributed to an unknown artist: *A painting is an arrangement of areas of color, within another given area, so as to produce a desired effect.* Other versions end in "greatest degree of emotion" or "so as to produce beauty." But I think "to produce a desired effect" is the best ending. The "meat" of the definition is in the beginning: *A painting is an arrangement of areas of color. That* is what you must abide by when you paint. You are not a camera or a recorder. You are speaking a new language. You are arranging areas of color. Sometimes you might want to change the definition to "a *drawing* is an arrangement of lines, values," etc. or "a sketch is an arrangement of areas of lights and darks," etc. The definition will help you think about what you are doing as a process, a means to an end, and not a copying exercise. *You* are the artist. *You* are speaking to the world. The best way to communicate is to let out your subconscious. To do this, use squiggles, doodles, or other methods of your own. Then translate through paint. When *you* are speaking, it doesn't matter what the subject is, as long as you speak your own way. Your clients will only love you more for being individual.

Once, while I was in Florida, I received a call from a young woman in Kentucky. She had bought my paintings before and now wanted me to do an abstract to go above her couch. We all know the "couch-size painting" jokes. But why not? (By the way, 30 x 40 inches is a good "couch size.") Why shouldn't a client ask for a "couch-size" painting? Michelangelo was constantly asked for a "cathedral-size" painting. My client proceeded to tell me the colors she wanted: deep blue, apricot, a little yellow, deep rust, parrot green. Oh, my. She sent me a swatch of her couch material and a color chip of her "off-white" wall.

I can see your hands flying up in horror. Where is the originality? Doesn't creativity count at all? Certainly it does. You can be as creative with someone else's ideas as you are with your own, perhaps even more so. The challenge is greater. Michelangelo almost always worked with someone else's desires in mind. Where was his originality? Don't I wish I had as much as he had? So, after my commission call, I went to work.

That dear woman had trusted me enough to commission me over the phone, certain that I could produce a painting that would please both of us. She said she wanted an original Piersol.

I let my imagination roam. I took out my squiggles. I thought of blues and apricots and off-white. Parrot green? Some bright white might add interest. She had not confined me to her colors; she just wanted each of hers used. My thoughts kept returning to the ocean which I could hear in the background. I found a squiggle that suited.

Digging out some magazines and old brochures from other artists, I selected pictures produced in grays – no color. I cut out sections of them in the values I wanted: light, medium, dark. I didn't cut out objects; just sections of tone. Then I tore those sections into pieces that fit my squiggle design pattern, keeping it all small enough to fit into a little design about 3½ x 5 inches. I find it easier to create designs by working small and without a brush in my hand. My brush is for rendering large flows of paint on the finished product. My fascination with what the brush does sometimes hinders my design sense.

After I had my little "paper piece" design, I pasted it down and made three photocopies of it – one for my client and two for me (a spare). If my little pasted-up design came apart, nothing was lost. All the design planning was done in grays, black, and white; no color. When satisfied with the design, I went to work, faithfully transferring it to the correct proportion on a large piece of gesso-coated masonite.

Was I creating? I certainly was. My painting was totally my own. My client felt she had participated and indeed she had, but the painting was mine, all mine. No matter how uninteresting a commission may seem, it becomes exciting as your own creativity takes over. Your work plan is the means by which you channel and use your creativity.

Discipline – simply making yourself work – is the key to success. The way to do that is to set up a work plan and stick to it religiously. Do whatever it takes to force yourself to work. Starving is a good incentive. If you arrange your life so that you have to survive on what your paint brush produces, you have given yourself the best present you will ever receive: incentive. Incentive breeds discipline; discipline breeds success.

Chapter Four

Creating a Successful Image

What is your image? It is how people perceive you. Create a successful image for yourself; build it from your credentials.

Start your image with a *résumé* (sometimes called a vitae or bio). You will give this to prospective clients and other people who ask for information about you. Write the résumé from the credits you have recorded on your record sheet.

Prepare your actual résumé when you have enough credits to fill about three-quarters of a page (they can be double spaced and stretched a little). Have it neatly typed or, better yet, printed. The classier it looks, the better. Don't skimp. Don't try to save money. Any time you do a promotion piece, even a résumé, make it represent the artist you are. Your best bet is a professional printing job, done in an exciting, easy-to-read typeface. If you are a good designer, you might do the layout yourself, but it is better to have it done by a specialist. Even if you are a graphic designer, another designer can present you better. A surgeon does not operate on himself. Remember, you are an artist and want to look like the best.

The résumé should not be more than two pages long, so choose the most exciting things you have done. State them in a way that will impress. Be positive. For instance, don't say, "I taught a few classes in watercolor at an art center." Instead, say, "Instructed watercolor classes at the North Hills Art Center." Get some professional help, either

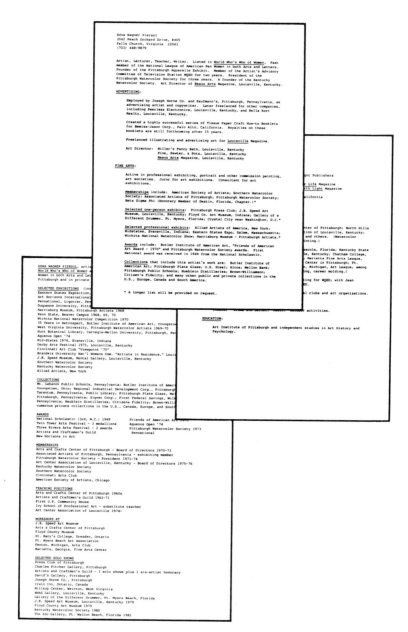

Edna Wagner Piersol
2042 Peach Orchard Drive, #405
Falls Church, Virginia 22043
(703) 448-9879

Artist, Lecturer, Teacher, Writer. Listed in World Who's Who of Women. Past
member of the National League of American Pen Women in both Arts and Letters.
Founder of the Pittsburgh Aquarelle Exhibit. Member of the Artist's Advisory
Committee of Television Station WQED for two years. President of the
Pittsburgh Watercolor Society for three years. A founder of the Kentucky
Watercolor Society. Art Director of Beaux Arts Magazine, Louisville, Kentucky.

ADVERTISING:

Employed by Joseph Horne Co. and Kaufmann's, Pittsburgh, Pennsylvania, as
advertising artist and copywriter. Later freelanced for other companies,
including Peerless Electronics, Louisville, Kentucky, and Rella Kort
Realty, Louisville, Kentucky.

Created a highly successful series of Tissue Paper Craft How-to Booklets
for Bemiss-Jason Corp., Palo Alto, California. Royalties on these
booklets are still forthcoming after 15 years.

Freelanced illustrating and advertising art for Louisville Magazine.

Art Director: Miller's Fancy Bath, Louisville, Kentucky
Pine, Pewter, & Pots, Louisville, Kentucky
Beaux Arts Magazine, Louisville, Kentucky

FINE ARTS:

Active in professional exhibiting, portrait and other commission painting,
art societies. Juror for art exhibitions. Consultant for art
exhibitions.

Memberships include: American Society of Artists; Southern Watercolor
Society; Associated Artists of Pittsburgh; Pittsburgh Watercolor Society;
Beta Sigma Phi (Honorary Member of Destin, Florida, Chapter.)*

Selected one-person exhibits: Pittsburgh Press Club; J.B. Speed Art
Museum, Louisville, Kentucky; Floyd Co. Art Museum, Indiana; Gallery of a
Different Drummer, Ft. Myers, Florida; Crystal City near Washington, D.C.*

Selected professional exhibits: Allied Artists of America, New York;
Midstates, Evansville, Indiana; Eastern States Expo, Salem, Massachusetts;
Wichita National Watercolor Show; Harrisburg Museum - Pittsburgh Artists.*

Awards include: Butler Institute of American Art, "Friends of American
Art Award - 1970" and Pittsburgh Watercolor Society awards. First
National award was received in 1949 from the National Scholastic.

Collections that include this artist's work are: Butler Institute of
American Art; Pittsburgh Plate Glass; U.S. Steel; Alcoa; Mellon Bank;
Pittsburgh Public Schools; Hueblein Distilleries; Brown-Williamson;
Citizen's Fidelity; and many other public and private collections in the
U.S., Europe, Canada and South America.

* A longer list will be provided on request.

EDUCATION:

Art Institute of Pittsburgh and independent studies in Art History and
Psychology.

EDNA WAGNER PIERSOL, arti
World Who's Who of Women a
Women in both Arts and Let
Pittsburgh and in private

SELECTED EXHIBITIONS (inv
Eastern States Exposition,
Art Horizons International
Pennational, Ligonier, Pen
Duquesne University, Pitts
Harrisburg Museum, Pittsburgh Artists 1968
Penn State, Beaver Campus 1968, 69, 70
Wichita National Watercolor Competition 1970
35 Years in Retrospect, Butler Institute of American Art, Youngsto
West Virginia University, Pittsburgh Watercolor Artists 1969-70
Hunt Botanical Library, Carnegie-Mellon University, Pittsburgh, Pen
Aqueous Open '74
Mid-States 1974, Evansville, Indiana
Derby Arts Festival 1975, Louisville, Kentucky
Cincinnati Art Club "Viewpoint '75"
Brandeis University Nat'l Womens Com. "Artists in Residence," Loui
J.B. Speed Museum, Rental Gallery, Louisville, Kentucky
Southern Watercolor Society
Kentucky Watercolor Society
Allied Artists, New York

COLLECTIONS
Mt. Lebanon Public Schools, Pennsylvania; Butler Institute of Amer
Youngstown, Ohio; Regional Industrial Development Corp., Pittsburg
Tarentum, Pennsylvania, Public Library; Pittsburgh Plate Glass, Me
Pittsburgh, Pennsylvania; Signet Corp.; First Federal Savings, Wil
Pennsylvania; Hueblein Distilleries; Citizens Fidelity; Brown-Will
numerous private collections in the U.S., Canada, Europe, and Sout

AWARDS
National Scholastic (3rd, W.C.) 1949   Friends of American Ar
Twin Tower Arts Festival - 3 medallions   Aqueous Open '74
Three Rivers Arts Festival - 2 awards   Pittsburgh Watercolor Society 1973
Artists and Craftsmen's Guild   Pennational
New Horizons in Art

MEMBERSHIPS
Arts and Crafts Center of Pittsburgh - Board of Directors 1970-73
Associated Artists of Pittsburgh, Pennsylvania - exhibiting member
Pittsburgh Watercolor Society - President 1971-74
Art Center Association of Louisville, Kentucky - Board of Directors 1975-76
Kentucky Watercolor Society
Southern Watercolor Society
Cincinnati Arts Club
American Society of Artists, Chicago

TEACHING POSITIONS
Arts and Crafts Center of Pittsburgh 1960s
Artists and Craftsmen's Guild 1962-71
First U.P. Community House
Ivy School of Professional Art - substitute teacher
Art Center Association of Louisville 1974-

WORKSHOPS AT
J.B. Speed Art Museum
Arts & Crafts Center of Pittsburgh
Floyd County Museum
St. Mary's College, Dresden, Ontario
Ft. Myers Beach Art Association
Fenton, Michigan, Arts Club
Marietta, Georgia, Fine Arts Center

SELECTED SOLO SHOWS
Press Club of Pittsburgh
Charles Pitcher Gallery, Pittsburgh
Artists and Craftsmen's Guild - 3 solo shows plus 1 six-artist honorary
David's Gallery, Pittsburgh
Joseph Horne Co., Pittsburgh
Irwin Inn, Ontario, Canada
Millsop Center, Weirton, West Virginia
WHAS Gallery, Louisville, Kentucky
Gallery of the Different Drummer, Ft. Myers Beach, Florida
J.B. Speed Art Museum, Louisville, Kentucky 1979
Floyd County Art Museum 1979
Kentucky Watercolor Society 1980
The Zoo Gallery, Ft. Walton Beach, Florida 1981

ght Publishers

r Life Magazine
th Light Magazine

alifornia

nter of Pittsburgh; North Hills
tion of Louisville, Kentucky;
and others. (Watercolor
inting.)

acola, Florida; Kentucky State
le, Kentucky; Chatham College,
, Marietta Fine Arts League,
Center in Pittsburgh; Ft.
n, Michigan, Art League; among
ing, career molding.)

ting for WQED; with Jean
ED.

l clubs and art organizations.

activities.

My two-page résumé is neatly presented on standard 8½x11-inch paper and covers my
entire work history, touching only highlights of my fine art career. On it I note that a
longer list of my fine art accomplishments is available. The 8½x14-inch sheet focuses
entirely on my fine art career and lists important facts, such as awards I have won, exhibitions I have had, and collections that contain my paintings.

50

from résumé agencies (listed in the phone book) or books on the subject (available at public libraries).

You will need other printed pieces besides your résumé. Business cards, brochures on your expertise in a special area such as illustrations or portraits, and mailing cards for general use to keep reminding the world that you exist. You should also have letterhead *stationery* indicating the kind of artist you are. All of these pieces should be exciting and used to spread your talent around the world.

Your *business card* must have good design. Nothing will defeat your purpose more quickly than a card that looks as if it were made by an amateur artist. If you are using a picture of a painting on the card, use one that you have seen reduced to size. Be sure it holds up and looks as good after reduction as it did before. Don't trust a printer to tell you it will look good; he's not an artist. I'm a firm believer in specialists. Find a good designer for all of your printed pieces; he knows what will work. Your business card should contain your name and address, plus the word artist or illustrator (some title to indicate that you are an artist), and your phone number. Let the card be arty, but keep it simple and effective.

Brochures are very useful. I have two, one for workshops and another for portraits. Once every two years, I go over my brochures and have new ones made. From time to time I make up short runs of a brochure for a quick project like my historic home series. Never stint on these. It's better to print a good one every couple of years than to try to run off sloppy, mimeographed ones that do more harm than good.

A good brochure is one that contains some selling information. In other words, it is a sophisticated, strongly designed advertisement about you and your work. In it you will need a few photos of your work. Strongly contrasted black and white shots of your finished paintings are effective. You should also have a photo of yourself and you must include an address and phone number or the brochure will be useless. It isn't a good idea to include prices since they change. Instead, use a separate price sheet which can be printed more cheaply.

My *mailing cards* are multipurpose. I use them for notes to friends, as enclosures in letters, or to hand to clients. Whenever I finish a painting that I especially like or one of my paintings receives an award, I commemorate it by having a 5x7-inch black and white glossy photo made. Glossy photos are better for reproduction and can be reduced for use on any card size. I then have picture postcards printed with my newest painting.

Description of Available Workshops:

These are One-Day Workshops. 9:30 a.m. to 2:30 p.m. (longer time possible if requested.) Each workshop is a self-contained one-day study. Any combination of workshops can be scheduled to arrange a 2 to 5 day watercolor clinic. Two-day weekend sessions are very popular.

Facing the WHITE PAPER
Featuring the one-stroke watercolor

White paper . . . the great equalizer! Watercolorists have all fought it at one time or another. It requires attack. Edna Piersol has developed a way of attacking with one stroke that establishes the whole painting in one swoop of the brush. Beginning students are astounded and students at other levels learn much from this new approach.

In this workshop the teacher also covers the various other approaches to painting a watercolor. Simple exercises that teach the aforementioned will be given. Exercises designed to get the class in the mood to paint. Students will be told what pigments to use and how to apply them. They will be given certain things to complete in certain time periods . . . 4 or 5 minutes and sometimes as short as 30 seconds. Ms. Piersol finds that students make tremendous strides in learning by this method. But beginners, you need not be

frightened. It's fun! The exercises will cause the student to learn about: composing paintings; application of pigment; color; use of tools; kinds of paper; understanding abstract ideas . . . all without realizing it "'til the light dawns."

This workshop is for beginners to advanced. The instructor has developed a way of teaching that makes each student feel at ease and each learns at his own level.

Facing the COLOR in Watercolor

This one-day workshop is a take off on a seminar that Edna Piersol has been teaching at various colleges. Class will begin with exercises which teach color as it applies to watercolor and get you in the mood to paint. The approach will be the same as in "FACING THE WHITE PAPER," giving the student definite things to do in definite time periods, but the emphasis will be on COLOR which IS the most important ingredient in watercolor. Students will learn about the various properties of pigments; their degree of permanence and transparency, etc.; what warm and cool colors do. Exercises will be given to help the student understand application of color. Paper influence on color will be discussed. This is a self contained study and may be scheduled without any of the other workshops but it is a good follow up to "FACING THE WHITE PAPER."

This brochure is one I have used to promote workshops. It folds in half horizontally and has an eye-catching illustration, my name, address, and phone number on the cover. The written text describes and "sells" each workshop to potential students.

This is an example of a brochure I use for clients interested in portraits. It folds vertically and includes my philosophy of portraiture.

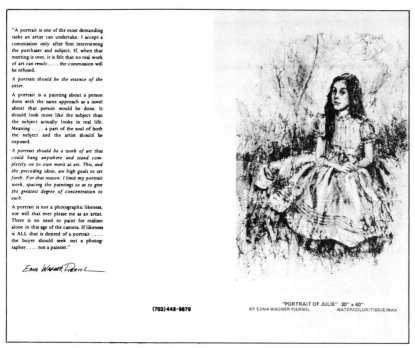

"A portrait is one of the most demanding tasks an artist can undertake. I accept a commission only after first interviewing the purchaser and subject. If, when that meeting is over, it is felt that no real work of art can result . . . . the commission will be refused.

A portrait should be the essence of the sitter.

A portrait is a painting about a person done with the same approach as a novel about that person would be done. It should look more like the subject than the subject actually looks in real life. Meaning . . . . a part of the soul of both the subject and the artist should be exposed.

A portrait should be a work of art that could hang anywhere and stand completely on its own merit as art. This, and the preceding ideas, are high goals to set forth. For that reason: I limit my portrait work, spacing the paintings so as to give the greatest degree of concentration to each.

A portrait is not a photographic likeness, nor will that ever please me as an artist. There is no need to paint for realism alone in this age of the camera. If likeness is ALL that is desired of a portrait . . . . the buyer should seek out a photographer . . . . not a painter."

Edna Wagner Piersol

(703) 448-9879

"PORTRAIT OF JULIE" 30" x 40"
BY EDNA WAGNER PIERSOL   WATERCOLOR/TISSUE/WAX

Printing Procedures

For those of you who have never had any printing done, I'll take you through the basic processes. For more detailed information, there are books dealing with the specifics of the subject. An excellent one is the *Graphics Handbook* by Howard Munce.

First, you'll need a layout, a plan drawn to the actual size of the printing. Let's say that you have a 5x7-inch photo of one of your paintings, and you want to use it on a 3x5-inch mailing card. Of course it will not fit, but your printer can reduce it. How do you know what size to tell him to reduce it to? There is a simple way. Draw a 5x7-inch rectangle. Then draw a diagonal line through the rectangle, from bottom left to top right. Now, let's say that you want to show the painting on the left side of your 3x5-inch mailing card and have some room on the right for printing.

If your painting is horizontal, it needs to be reduced to about two and a half inches high in order to fit inside the card and allow a little margin. How much space will be left for printing? How wide will the reduced picture be? To find out, measure up the left side of your drawn rectangle to two and a half inches. Now draw a straight line, parallel to the base line, over to the diagonal line and another line straight down from the spot where the lines meet to the bottom of the rectangle. You now have the exact size of the reduction. Place the little rectangle on your layout, exactly where you want the picture. You'll now see the space left for your printing.

You will be able to tell from the printer's sample book what typeface looks good, but it is another matter to choose a type point size. The printer will know how small the point size has to be in order to get all of your wording to fit. If the type looks too small to you, you will have to eliminate some of the words. Let simplicity of design be the star; the fewer words you use, the larger they can be.

It will help you to know something about how a photograph is printed. In order to reproduce it, the printer must first shoot a negative of your photo. This negative is shot through a screen that breaks up your picture into little dots of various sizes to create halftone effects. Look at a newspaper picture with a magnifying glass and you will see the dots. (For a newspaper, the dots must be quite coarse.)

Knowing how the process works can help you to choose photographs of your work, ones that have good contrast. To decide what areas or fine lines might be lost in the printing process, squint at the photo with your eyes half closed. Anything you don't see is not likely to show up on the printed piece.

Only pictures with grays in them need screens. Line drawings do not require screens for printing; therefore, they are cheaper to reproduce. The printing of color photographs requires a separate screen for each basic color. To achieve a full-color effect, you need four screened negatives—red, yellow, blue and black, and four printing runs through the press. That gets expensive.

A way to get color into your printed pieces without a lot of extra cost is by using a colored ink for the entire printing. You can also use colored paper and colored ink – two colors for the price of one. Printers usually offer price breaks with larger quantities, so you may find it is almost as cheap to get two hundred brochures as one hundred, and probably as expensive to get ten as one hundred. At five hundred and more, you should receive further price breaks.

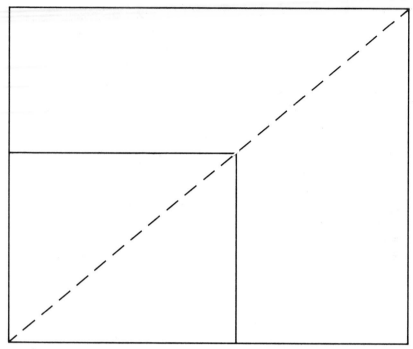
A reduction rectangle.

This basic printing information should be used as a guide to make you feel more confident about what you are doing, but I can't stress enough the advantages of professional help. Save yourself a lot of grief by finding a good photographer, printer, and graphic designer, and make use of all of them.

Presentation Tools

Once your printed pieces are available, you are ready to make a presentation to a potential client. Now you'll need some other tools.

A *briefcase-size portfolio* can be bought at most art supply stores. Mine is the 11x14-inch size. In it I have several 8x10-inch color photographs of paintings. Those photos are expensive, but I have as many paintings as possible photographed. Also in the briefcase are some small samples of drawings, newspaper clippings, and testimonial letters — all things that will impress clients. The briefcase has a pocket on either side to hold my brochures. As long as that portfolio is in my car, I'm ready at any moment to make a presentation.

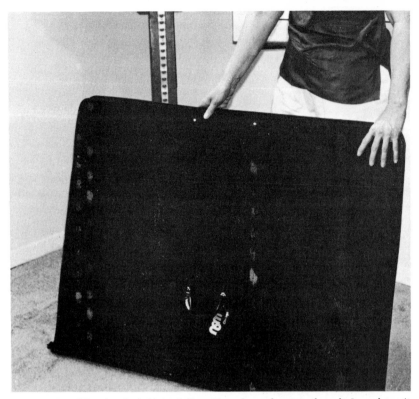

My large portfolio that I pack carefully with unframed, original work. I can have it ready and waiting for the time when a client expresses an interest in seeing some of my paintings. (Photo by Bob Young)

I also have a *large portfolio* for paintings, although I don't carry it with me at all times. When a client has expressed an interest in seeing actual work, I pack it carefully. I make the paintings look as good as possible without frames by using good-looking mats and a foam-core backing on each one to keep it straight. Each painting is wrapped in clear vinyl. This can be bought by the yard in the housewares department of a discount store. The vinyl I like is the kind used in making tablecloths, etc., since it is more supple than acetate. Also, it's usually cheaper. Whatever you use, the portfolio contents must be neat and organized.

Sometimes a slide viewer and 35mm color transparencies of your paintings work better than taking the actual work. I have a book for slides with clear vinyl pages containing twenty pockets per page. The slides can be organized according to subject and the pages held up to the light in a client's office so he can quickly see what he likes. The slides he chooses can then be shown on the small viewer you carry with you. Never make a client supply any equipment, such as a slide projector, but at the same time, never carry so much paraphernalia into his office as to be obtrusive. Be neat and well organized.

Telephoning Clients

At this point you should be ready for your big presentation. You have found a client by advertising or, perhaps, you are going to make what salesmen dub a "cold call." Let's take it from the top and walk through this one together.

Pick up the Yellow Pages of the phone directory and look at the ads for interior decorators. (Select one who can afford a large ad.) I've found that a good time of day to phone decorators is four in the afternoon. They are back in their offices and finished with clients for the day. This is another kind of research you have to do – finding good psychological times to approach people, but another book could be written on that.

Now, go ahead, dial his number.

("Jacob's Interiors.") It is a secretary or assistant.

"Hello, my name is (Edna Wagner Piersol); I am an artist and I've been associated with (Norcross Gallery in Cleveland) for a long time. I'm not a Sunday painter."

It is important to let the potential client know that you are a professional. In your introduction say the most exciting thing you can about yourself as an artist. Don't be shy. Say loud and clear, "I have recently won an award in the (Gulf Coast Art Show)," or "I'm listed in (*Who's Who of Artists*)." Stick to facts. Don't make up anything, but this stage is terribly important, so it is not the time to be modest either. Don't even think of saying something silly like "I call myself an artist." *Pick one or two of your most impressive accomplishments and state them.* Then say, "I am calling to inquire if your company ever purchases paintings directly from artists."

You will save a lot of time and effort by finding out this crucial point immediately. If you get a "yes" answer to your inquiry, you can then make an appointment to see the decorator and show your wares. If they say "no," go on to the next decorator in the Yellow Pages.

In-Person Calls

Sometimes instead of a "cold" telephone call I make a "cold" personal call, and these are always well thought out. I check out the shop in advance to determine if I think my paintings would go well with its other merchandise. Then I walk in with my portfolio of photos, etc., in one hand and a printed brochure in the other. I go so far as to fold the brochure in such a way that a photo will be sure to catch any interested eye. Be aware that you probably won't see "Mr. Big" at this moment. It will be his assistant, but walk in smiling and say, "Hello, I'm (Edna Wagner Piersol). I'm an artist."

Extend the printed brochure saying, "I've been selling to (Smith Decorators in Cleveland) for quite a while and I want to expand my market. Do you ever buy work directly from artists?"

In this case I have my big portfolio in the car packed with paintings that I think this particular client may like. But I do not take it into the shop until the introductions are over.

When you are talking to an assistant be just as friendly as you will be when you finally meet the boss. You want to impress him so that when he gives your brochure and message to "Mr. Big," he is in your corner already. Tell the assistant that you would like to see the owner or manager, and if you can't see him that day, find out when would be a good time to call for an appointment.

When you are finally granted an interview with a new client, it should go like this:

Walk in once again with your briefcase portfolio under your arm and a brochure in your hand. You should have the slide projector and slides neatly packed in a small bag, your portfolio in the car waiting.

"Hello," you say, extending your free hand. "I'm impressed by your shop and I'm delighted to meet you."

He can't help but smile. You have done nothing but compliment him.

Get to the point quickly, but don't rush so that you become tongue-tied. Take a deep breath. Pretend to yourself you are selling someone else's work. If he doesn't like yours, it's not your fault, or his either. This is the hardest part. Don't take offense.

Say, "The (Jones Interiors of Edinboro) has been purchasing my work for (two years) and I've also sold to decorators in (Atlanta and Louisville)." Say whatever you have done that may impress him.

Avoid negatives, and don't try to be modest.

While you are talking, open your small portfolio and show him some photos of you work. Tell him that you have a portfolio of original paintings out in the car. Say, "I'll go out and get them," and go, if he doesn't stop you. Don't say, "I'll get them if you'd like to see them." That gives him a chance to tell you he is busy.

Bring in your large case and get out your paintings – five or six will do. Say something to indicate the price of your work. I've found it helpful to play my price off against higher prices in other cities or higher-priced artists. You might say, "As you know, original art can have prices as high as ($350), but when I'm selling mine, unframed, in quantity, I am willing to sell them for ($125) per painting. They will be matted and wrapped in vinyl for protection. As far as quantity goes, you can have them in lots of (four)." Don't belabor this. Just get in your tiny sales pitch as fast as you can. Stand back and beam as though you had won a lottery. Let's hope he is intrigued. If he's not pleased, leave as quickly and as gracefully as you can and look for another client. And don't get discouraged.

I've been taking you through a presentation to an interior decorator, but there are other types of businesses that buy original art. For large corporations you should vary your technique. There you should not suggest quantity buying. Instead, say that you would like your paintings in their collections, that you would be happy to sell your work unframed so they can select the frame. Try selling your work to individual collectors, banks, and furniture stores. Let them all know that you are willing to work on commission basis. Slant your presentation for each client's individual needs. Keep records on what they say; if they ask you to come back in one month or six months, *do* it. Write it on your calendar and *don't* forget.

About now, you may realize that it would help to have an agent. Yes, but they are hard to come by. Prospective agents are a dime a dozen, but *good* agents must really know you and your art. To be good they must be almost able to think like you. Even if you find a suitable agent, you will have to offer considerable guidance. It is more desirable to learn to be your own agent. Better yet, involve a spouse or close relative in your work or hire other help to take the pressure off of yourself. I find a secretary very useful and I'm living for the day when I can have one full-time. Perhaps a studio assistant can lighten your work load so that your mind can be freer. I never do anything that does not require me personally, but I've never found a substitute for personal contact with art buyers.

Your Special Image

Image is how others perceive us. However, to be effective at anything, you must first perceive yourself as special. Be aware that there are things about you and your art that are different from anyone else. Learn what they are by listening carefully to what viewers say about your work. Play up your specialty in all your brochures and promotions. Then find out who needs your kind of work and go after them.

The thrust of this book is not to teach you how to be a fine artist. I'm trying to help you make money with your art – enough money to support yourself, and remain true to yourself. When you are famous and no longer have to worry about money, you will not regret your actions during your years of struggle.

Remain true to yourself, but be as interesting as possible to others. No matter what type of personality you are, there is a way to use it to your advantage. Even if you are painfully shy, you can seem mysterious, and it will be an advantage if played upon in the right light. Professional help in writing your printed pieces is so helpful because another specialist in his trade can be objective and bring out your best qualities.

Build yourself a good image. Show yourself to the best advantage.

Chapter Five

Outdoor Exhibitions and Sales

There is a pattern to the way an artist should develop and mature in exhibiting. This is the path I'd suggest:

• Nonjuried local shows and outdoor shows
• Juried shows
• Small one-person shows and/or cooperative gallery shows
• Small galleries
• Big galleries
• Museum one-person shows
• Sales to corporations and commissions.

It goes without saying that you must be flexible. This schedule might be changed by good fortune. You may receive commissions much ahead of my scheduling.

A good way to get your exhibiting feet wet is through outdoor shows. Business-wise, they are relaxed, and you'll benefit by talking to the public. Art magazines often list exhibit opportunities. Many outdoor shows are nonjuried and you may want to try those first. That way you won't face rejection by a jury along with the rest of any misgivings you may have about showing your work. The first time you show your paintings in public you cannot help but feel naked. Every artist does. It is something you learn to live with. In most nonjuried outdoor shows you will pay a fee for space. The higher the fee, the more exposure you should expect. Sometimes the fee is charged on a percentage of sales. This is my favorite kind of arrangement.

All shows send out a printed *prospectus* on request. This is your set of instructions and should be considered your bible for that particular event. Don't try to bend the rules. If the committee requires that you arrive between ten and noon, rearrange your life so that you can be there then. If the prospectus says space will be given on a first-come basis, arrive at eight for a ten o'clock entry time. Get your parking space and do whatever you can for your comfort beforehand. I have never yet managed to be first at the entry line. Artists experienced in outdoor showing are early birds.

Keep records from year to year on each show in a notebook that is just for this purpose. Keep details about the time you arrived, where you parked, what time you actually finished setting up, when the first browser arrived, what time you made your first sale, and when *any-one* made a first sale. Try to find out how many sales were made and the sizes of the sold paintings. Did abstracts sell more than realism? Write it all down. You'll love yourself next year. Keep a record of expenses, too; operate as a business.

Organizing Your Display

Once again, organization is your best ally. You will need upright display units and a display bin; the units hold framed paintings and the bin holds unframed works. Both need to be portable. Take a look at what other artists use. Visit an outdoor show before you exhibit, making notes on everything the artists do.

The display units can be built from conduit and wire mesh. A good design is an A-frame type: two squares of conduit formed into frames covered with wire mesh, then hinged together at the top with wire. The frames should measure about forty inches wide and sixty inches tall, but they can have removable legs so that the frames will fit into a station wagon. Other units are made from peg board or are wooden frames stretched with chicken wire. These constructions can stand up in the manner of room dividers. There are many other ingenious designs you will find used by artists in outdoor shows.

You should have a bin for your unframed work. A good type is a folding container like the one pictured. It folds to fit in your car or van, and opens to hold fifty or so sketches.

Cover your sketches with acetate or, better yet, clear vinyl you can buy by the yard. Your work will be well-protected from the elements this way. People can handle the sketches without ruining hundreds of dollars' worth of your work with fingerprints. I mount my sketches on heavy mounting board or museum board. After mounting, a piece of vinyl is cut about six inches larger than the sketch. On the back of the sketch, I lay a double thickness of brown paper. Then tape the vinyl to the paper after folding it around the painting. This saves money and provides protection from moisture. If you run into a really rainy day you may wish you had wrapped the whole picture in vinyl and spent a little more money.

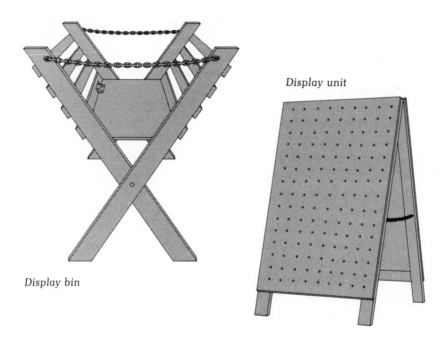

Display unit

Display bin

Surviving the Elements

On the show circuit, rain is something you must contend with – and sometimes you do contend! It's best to prepare for that possibility right from the start. Rain clouds have been known to travel hundreds of miles out of their way just to attend an outdoor art exhibit. Always carry a tarpaulin with you to your booth. Have some plastic garbage bags on hand; you can stick all of your paintings and paraphernalia into them in an emergency.

Set up your display in such a way that you can get the paintings off the panels and into bags quickly. Paintings can survive rain pretty well in bags leaning upright against the bin under the tarp. Have a rain drill – the way you used to have a fire drill in school. Plan the quickest way to get your work to your car. Have your browse bin built so that there is an opening in the bottom to let rain water drain out. Keep a rain slicker with your show equipment. Who knows? It may keep the rain away.

Wooden dowels about a half an inch in diameter and about the width of your bin should be kept in the bottom of your browse bin. When it's time to stack your paintings, lay the dowels down first and stack the painting across them. This keeps the artwork away from any wet at the bottom.

There are *price tags* and *sales records* to consider. Price tags can be stickers you find in office supply stores. It's best to clearly mark a price and not to negotiate each one. I know it's tempting to just let people make offers or try to juggle your prices to suit the clientele, but don't. Base your price on facts. How much do you realistically need to get from the pieces? After you have decided that and marked the paintings plainly, you can quietly come down on a price if a customer asks, and you are willing.

When marking the tags, think again of rain and moisture. Use waterproof ink. Keep part of your show record notebook for a record of sales. Record the sale, the price, the title and size of the painting, the time of day it sold, and the *name and address of the buyer*. These records are priceless. You will be able to discern patterns of buying habits that will help you to analyze sales. You need the name and address of the buyer for mailings about your next showings.

Most problems of outdoor exhibiting can be anticipated and solved before they happen. We've talked about rain, but there is also sun – almost equally as devastating to paintings and to you. Find an exhibit space in the shade if you can. Rig some kind of sun shade. This is hard to do without destroying visibility of the paintings. Take folding lawn chairs with you, and find a way to attach sun umbrellas to them. Beach equipment sometimes works well. One year I took my large picnic table umbrella and set it up in such a way as to shade the whole display. It worked surprisingly well and we moved it several times during the day. An ice chest is another comfort must.

Here is a checklist of the things needed for an outdoor show:

- Notebook (for records)
- Display unit
- Display bin for matted, unframed pieces
- Vinyl for covering paintings
- Tarpaulin
- Large plastic garbage bags
- Dowels for browse bin
- Rain slicker
- Price stickers
- Indelible ink pen
- Folding lawn chairs
- Food, refreshments
- Ice chest
- Picture wire
- Masking tape
- Drapery hooks to hang paintings on display unit
- Large pieces of cardboard to slip between paintings while carrying
- An assistant to man your booth while you take breaks

Outdoor exhibiting can be an enjoyable experience. You must go armed with a sense of humor. Listening to the public's comments is a unique experience. The different attitudes that people have about artists have always intrigued me. I once listened while someone who was familiar with my work, but who did not know me by sight, explained why I was in my *Onion Period*. I didn't even know I was in an *Onion Period*. I just didn't have the courage to tell the viewer that he was talking to the artist; I was too fascinated to hear his views to stop him. Then, after he'd gone so far, I couldn't think of a way to tell him without bursting into laughter. I spent the rest of the show furtively glancing around to make sure he did not come upon me unawares and find out who I really was.

Painting for the Crowd

Many artists demonstrate their painting techniques at their booths. I don't do much of this anymore, but I do sketch a lot. When an artist is sitting and sketching with pen and pad, people always come up to look and good conversations begin. In fact, my favorite trick in getting to know people anywhere is to take a small sketch book and sit on a wall at an outdoor concert, or lean against my car on some historic street, and sketch. People stop, look through the book and say, "What would you charge for a painting done from this sketch?" I've sold many a commission from my sketch book. I've even sketched at parties. I'm not an exhibitionist and I never do it when I feel the occasion is too formal. But, I feel whole with a pencil or pen in my hand. I feel at ease and that puts others at ease. If you demonstrate at shows, be prepared to be interrupted. Do something that is easy and fun for you; don't tackle a masterpiece.

Outdoor shows are the best way in the world to pay your dues as an artist. They prepare you for better things to come, and from them you will learn things about handling yourself as an artist that you can't learn anywhere else.

Some artists find outdoor shows to be their main source for sales. The following interview is with a Louisville, Kentucky, artist who has been very successful at outdoor shows.

Kathryn Witte
Artist
Louisville, Kentucky

Q. You are a successful art fair exhibitor. I know that you choose to be selective regarding your shows and to live a slow-paced life. Still you are successful and probably could make any amount of money you desire. Would you share your thoughts on art fairs with us?
A. Don't belittle the importance of art fairs for making money as an artist. Fairs are a way of making quick cash sales as well as good contacts for future sales. Remember, this is a fun venture to be enjoyed with the public. Be well-organized before the opening day. Keep everything as simple as possible. Paintings should be matted, covered with acetate, and priced. Personally, I take only work that I am proud of – not the failures to sell cheap.

Since I have no help in setting up my booth, I make it easy for me. My bin (homemade) folds up and fits in my car trunk. I use two or three pegboards (A-line) for display. I always take two folding

Winter Enchantment, 30x40 inches, monoprint, by Kathryn Witte.

chairs – one is for the tired visitor. That chair always faces my paintings and usually the visit ends in a purchase.

Q. How many paintings do you take to a show?

A. I think too many pictures in a booth boggles the mind of the buyer. Be selective. Display only a few of your best at a time. As you sell, put others out.

Q. What is your best hint for success to beginning fair exhibitors?

A. Enjoy yourself! I think this is one of the secrets of a successful venture. Talk, laugh, and kid with the people. People come to the fairs to be entertained as well as to buy. Time your talking with them to be after they have shown sufficient interest in your work. You soon learn that every person who passes your booth is not a prospective buyer. Beware of looking bored or reading a book. And remember to stay until the closing hour; many sales are made then.

Q. Any last parting bit of advice?

A. Good luck!

Chapter Six

Juried
Art
Exhibitions

When are you ready to enter a juried show? That is an exhibit that has a judge or jury to accept or reject your painting and to give awards. Jury information plus all the other regulations are always printed in a brochure about the show called a *prospectus*. You are ready to enter these shows as soon as you are ready to sell paintings and want to find out what the rest of the world thinks of your work.

To find juried shows, watch your newspaper for local opportunities and read the art magazines for shows in the rest of the country.

First, send for the prospectus. Deadlines for entering are months ahead of show time, so be prepared to think far in advance. When you get the prospectus, read it carefully and do whatever it requires for entry. Usually the prospectus will ask you to submit color transparencies of your work. Read the eligibility section, so you won't enter acrylic-coated caseins in a watercolor show demanding work on paper and unvarnished. Select your best work by the photographic slide, not by the original, since the jury will see only the slide. Pay attention to the size limitations listed on the prospectus and stick to the framing regulations. Fill out the entry blank that comes with the prospectus.

Paying attention to detail will not insure your acceptance into the show. Nothing can do that, but you can save yourself a lot of grief by being meticulous. Prove you are a pro even if it is your first experience. Your first show can be a traumatic experience. Whatever happens to you, be it good or bad, will probably be reversed in your second show or soon thereafter. Be prepared for many ups and downs; they will continue as long as you are exhibiting.

Understanding the System

Find out how shows work by volunteering to help. Work on as many exhibit committees as you can. You will soon see that the problems involved in selecting work and hanging shows make it almost impossible to be fair. In this case, it's better to try to think negatively for a change. Don't expect to get into shows. Don't hope to win awards. Consider it all a learning experience, somewhat like gambling. Then when a good thing comes along it will be wonderful.

If you are rejected, remember that your rejection comes from the personality of the juror, not necessarily from the quality of your work. When there is exhibit space for sixty paintings and the show committee finds three hundred entries on their hands, you know that some very good work has to lose out. What would you do, if you were the juror, after you have "thrown out" all the work that you feel is weak and you still have two hundred good paintings facing you with only sixty spaces available? As a juror, you may be tempted to flip a coin. Even then, the first time around, you'll only get rid of 50 percent of the paintings, and you still have to eliminate forty more in some way. The problems faced by exhibit committees and jurors are monumental.

Back when I entered almost every show that came along, I used to keep a record of what happened to my work under each juror. Then, when I faced that juror again, I'd know what he liked or did not like when he last saw my work. No one gives you a report on what happened to your work. No one can possibly tell you why the juror did not select your offering. You have to figure these things out for yourself from whatever pattern you discern. If you work on the show committee, you have a chance of overhearing things that will help you make decisions about your work. But, even when you do hear something a juror says about your work, you have not exactly heard the word of God; the next juror may feel differently. After a while, you begin to take it all with a grain of salt and come to realize that you only compete with yourself.

Don't give up on entering the shows. It is one of the best ways to grow as an artist. When you are successful in one area, move up to more prestigious shows with better artists. The day will come when you no longer have time to enter every show. Later, when you are well known, you may have no time for shows at all. But if you haven't taken your knocks in exhibits, and paid your dues, how will you ever let the world know you exist?

Completing the Picture

There are some extra things you can do, besides creating good art, that will help your chances in a show. One is good framing. I've heard juror after juror complain about the bad frames many artists use. A frame is an integral part of the painting. The nicest frame I ever saw was on a John Marin painting that still hangs over the fireplace in the room in his studio-home at Cape Split, Maine, where he died. He made the frame at the same time he created the painting. It is rough hewn and covered with the same paint as the painting. It is such a work of art that I felt I was looking at a painting that turned into sculpture at the frame's edge. A frame should always be subordinate to the painting and never overpower it. You cannot always trust a framer to do it right. You must tell him exactly what you want. It's up to you to choose the frame and the mat color.

Slides, Shipping and Fees

Today, jurors only look at slides to judge most shows. Of course, the frame should not be included in the photograph. There are ways you can help yourself when faced with slide jurying. Be sure the slide is clear and sharp and has enough contrast to grab the eye. Photograph the painting straight on, so it is square on the slide. If any background shows on the transparency, block it out with silver tape that you can buy in photography shops. Follow religiously the prospectus directions for labeling. When choosing the slides to enter, I check mine against good slides of other artists' paintings. I acquire as many slides of the work of artist friends as I can – artists who are frequently successful in shows. If my slide holds up well against theirs, it has a better chance to hold up against other good artists in the next show.

Shipping the accepted pictures to shows can be a headache. Check out United Parcel Service (UPS), air freight, and Greyhound to find out the size limit on shipments. When you send a painting by UPS, or some other shipping service, they will ask you what is inside. Tell them that it is artwork, without glass, and is replaceable by money. That is an answer that meets all of their requirements except size. You may need to have a crate to assure safe handling. Sometimes you can get mirror boxes from furniture stores that are a big help. Some artists solve shipping problems by helping one another. They ship paintings to each other unframed and take them to framers in their own towns for each other. Vanning art is also becoming popular. If you belong to an art group with several artists who are sending paintings to the same show, think of joining together to hire a van and driver.

How about the fees for juried shows? They are necessary to pay the juror and exhibit space rent, plus other show expenses, and are not refundable. When your work is not accepted in a show, consider the fee as your contribution to the welfare of the art world.

Checklist for exhibiting in juried shows:

- Send for prospectus of as many shows as you can
- Return entry blanks, slides, and fees on time
- Mark dates of shipping, jurying, returns, etc.
- Proper framing (sturdy for shipping)
- Good color slides of your artwork
- Shipping crates (made with strong sides)
- Plexiglas (or some other unbreakable, transparent material) on paintings instead of glass

Entering a juried show can be the most challenging and the most frightening step you take in your career. Your first show will be remembered all your life after others have blurred. It's hard. The best way to go at it is not to think about it. Enter shows as though you were performing a ritual. At least you won't be executed if you're not accepted. Don't consider rejection as failure; consider the whole thing an experiment. It's a lot like horse racing – get yourself to the starting gate.

The following interview with an experienced show juror lists reasons why a painting might be accepted or rejected during the jurying process. Also, read it for additional information on why juried outdoor shows are good for artists to enter.

Bernice Osborne
Past President
Southern Watercolor Society
Gulf Breeze, Florida

Q. You have juried many exhibits and served on numerous steering committees for art shows and festivals. What do you look for when jurying a show?
A. The key things are originality and concept, especially a painting that is novel or wonderfully naive.
Q. What is your most frequent reason for accepting a painting for exhibit?
A. There are a lot of reasons for accepting paintings and visual impact is probably the first. A painting that holds up twelve to twenty feet from the juror has a good chance – a painting that makes a statement from across the room. If you really want to get technical, I think that *value* is the particular design element that produces impact.

Other very good reasons are the imaginative use of technique and facility. A painting that causes the viewer to want to go up and touch it, that causes the question to be asked, "How was that done?" is often, in my opinion, a good painting.

Another reason (and perhaps more important than the previous ones) is discovering a painting that produces feeling, makes a statement within itself – a totality of expression like a book or a song.
Q. What most often causes an artist's paintings to be rejected?
A. Lack of facility, I'd say; sloppy presentation, such as poorly

Shadows of My Mind, 28x36 inches, watercolor, by Bernice Osborne.

matted paintings or nowadays, as we enter so many shows by slides, unprofessional slides. Bad slides harm many artists' chances. I like to use this analogy: A woman makes a beautiful dress and then presents it without the hem. That's what an artist does when a painting is presented in an unprofessional way. Another reason for failure is the inability to be original.

Q. How early in a career should an artist begin to enter exhibits?

A. As soon as he feels good about his work. An artist should ask someone he respects for an opinion. Ask a former teacher, one who exhibits. See what several successful artists think of the total work. When you lack assurance, seek wisdom. Some artists do enter shows too soon but that contributes to their education. The artists I worry about are the ones who hold back from entering shows after they really are ready. Exhibiting is part of an artist's career. The inability to accept one's own contribution and what one has to say is something each artist has to come to grips with.

Q. Do you think jurors rely on their personal tastes to judge work?

A. Absolutely.

Q. Do you think that is bad?

A. No, I think it is wonderful. I think that's what makes an artist/juror good. It's inevitable that everything that has influenced an artist up to the point when he becomes a juror will go into his decision. To me, that's good.

Q. I know that you have been on the steering committee for a large outdoor art festival. You helped to decide how to jury the show. What advice do you have for would-be exhibitors in outdoor shows?

A. The best thing about outdoor shows is that they help to establish an artist in the community. They are stepping stones to broadening a career.

Q. Are the rules for presentations different from the rules for group shows or museum shows?

A. Good presentation is good presentation anywhere, but in outdoor shows be very careful about *total* presentation. It's important to give a concise viewing of your work. Have a total concept. This gets people to look at your work and probably accomplishes better sales.

Chapter Seven

Exhibiting
in Galleries

There are as many kinds of galleries as there are artists. There are commercial galleries and sophisticated galleries, each with its own clientele and price range. Some galleries are in business to make money, some are tax write-offs. Your challenge is to find one that will benefit you, regardless of the gallery's motives.

You will probably start exhibiting in one of the less sophisticated galleries and then move on to better ones. It is best to start in one small town and then graduate to bigger galleries in larger towns until you are exhibiting where you want to be – New York, Chicago, San Francisco, Washington, D.C. That way there are no hard feelings created by changing galleries in the same town.

You can wait to be discovered in a local exhibit or you can build up a portfolio to make a presentation, such as I took you through earlier. The latter is the better approach. Don't wait to have good things happen. Instead, *make* things happen. Start by phoning some of the galleries in your area. Ask whether they are accepting new artists. Tell them what they need to know about you. Find out what kind of art they like, but *never change your style for a gallery.* You can be influenced by what others think, but when you change your style of painting, it should be because of some natural growth coming from within yourself. I've stressed this before, but I can't say it enough. Whenever you seek other's opinions, always weigh their advice against your own thoughts. Keep yourself open and in a growth process. This is particularly important in dealing with a gallery. Try to find a gallery that fits your own style.

Going to the galleries in person is sometimes better than phone calls. You can walk in and browse without even suggesting you are an artist. See if your work belongs there. Perhaps you will feel so good about the place that you will want to introduce yourself before you leave and make an appointment to show your work to the director.

Be prepared for surprises when you make your presentation. Sometimes there's a great rapport from the start, but even now, with my work in several galleries and museums, I sometimes encounter a negative response from a new gallery. It's a puzzling experience. One director had told me that my work did not appeal to his clientele. Strange – I had looked at the paintings on his gallery's walls and felt that several of the works were close to my kind of painting, but I didn't argue with him. I liked this gallery enough that I asked for a chance to show him some other types of artwork. He agreed. However, it is best not to try to beat a dead horse. I may or may not go back. I'll think about it, but I *will* go on to seek other galleries. For every artist, there is a gallery, many galleries, that will be glad to try to sell that artist's work.

Cooperative Galleries

Cooperative galleries are a comfortable way for an artist to enter the exhibiting arena. Many cities have art centers run by artists. In my formative years, I was accepted by the Arts and Crafts Center of Pittsburgh – a very professional group, and it was extremely good for my career. An artist must first be professionally screened by his peers to be accepted by one of the member groups, such as Associated Artists of Pittsburgh or the Society of Sculptors. After that, an artist has the right to exhibit in the galleries and teach at the teaching center, and must work for the organization. Members are expected to put in time selling and cleaning, and to handle all the chores connected with an art center.

In Washington, D.C., there is an interesting group of artists in the Torpedo Factory Art Center. The Torpedo Factory is run in a way different from the Pittsburgh group. After being accepted, one rents studio space and works there a certain number of hours each week. The artist exhibits from his own studio.

The following interviews, one with the director of the Torpedo Factory Art Center and another with an artist who exhibits there, point out the specific advantages to cooperative studio space.

Marge Alderson
Director
The Torpedo Factory Art Center
Alexandria, Virginia

Q. You are the director of an artist's cooperative and are an artist also. You must be well informed about what the world wants from an artist.
A. Yes, I'm a watercolorist; and yes, I spend a lot of time on art professionalism.
Q. Why would collective studio space be advantageous to an artist?
A. For the cost of rental space in our center, the artist achieves these goals: a place to work; a place to sell; a place to interact with other artists; a place to compete and exhibit; and, a place to teach and study since there is an art school here.

All this, plus the fact that this center is publicly owned and provides reasonable rental space, makes this an attractive alternative to private studio space.
Q. How does an artist go about acquiring space here?
A. You apply by coming in and inquiring. An artist will be asked to submit work to a panel of three judges – top professionals who are not connected with the center. Judges are selected through recommendations of members of the center, who suggest the names of top people in their fields. I direct the jury to choose artists with work comparable to, or better than, art already in the center. Our jury is made up of artists knowledgeable in three-dimensional work, two-dimensional work, and fine crafts. Screening takes place two times a year.

The Cypress, 41x40 inches, watercolor, by Marge Alderson.

Q. What is the biggest stumbling block for an artist facing the jury?
A. Presentation. Poor or inappropriate matting, i.e., colored mats, sloppy framing – matting and framing are not taught enough. But there are places an artist can learn. I've discovered that frame-it-yourself places do teach this and have a lot of good information, but they are not slanted toward the prejudices of jurors in the art world. An artist should show his pride in his work by the way he presents it. It shouldn't say, I just tossed this off. It should be professional.
Q. Please define the word professional, as a juror would.
A. For passing a jury, more than anything else, it's attitude – an attitude that denotes experience. The way an artist presents his work

reflects knowledge of accepted standards and disciplined personal direction toward improvement.

Q. To be a professional artist you need to do more than pass a jury from time to time, wouldn't you say?

A. Yes, and believe it or not, the Internal Revenue Service (IRS) provides a good guideline as to what a professional artist must do. If an artist is not doing those things, he's probably not yet a pro. [IRS Publication 334, *Tax Guide for Small Businesses*, can be obtained free of charge from any IRS office.]

Clay Huffman
Artist
The Torpedo Factory Art Center
Alexandria, Virginia

Q. What made you decide to go on your own as a screen printer and open up a studio?

A. I had always wanted to be an artist of some kind. I started when I was fourteen; not full-time, of course. I took architecture in college, but was turned off after two years. I went back to doing pottery as I had been doing in high school. Then I took some lessons in screen printing at The Torpedo Factory and the prints began to sell well.

Q. Did you start right in being a full-time artist?

A. No, a recession started, so I tried to get into another profession. I went to computer school and got a job which I thought I enjoyed. But after three months I went back to art full-time. That's when I opened up the studio at The Torpedo Factory.

Q. What caused you to go back to art?

A. In art I have more control. If something bad happens (financially), all I have to do is to put more energy into it to make it turn out well.

Q. How do you handle your finances otherwise?

A. I live in a group house; sharing expenses helps. I pay bills as the money comes in. I've learned a lot about the art retail sales market. September is the worst month for selling here. [Alexandria is a tourist town just across the Potomac River from Washington, D.C.] Christmas is sometimes good, but you can't count on it. If December is bad, January will usually turn out okay. Summer drops off. You have to go through a year or two, wherever you are selling, to find the pattern, and then you can judge your budget better. My inventory of any one print sells in two or three years. Each edition is about ninety prints.

Q. How do you like the cooperative studio idea?

A. It's great. I like having other artists around. The interaction is great. If it wasn't for the art center, I couldn't make it financially.

Q. How long do you work at a time?

A. About fifteen hours per day for five or six days per week. I used to work longer, but now I control my time better. I'm more established.

Q. Do you work on commission?

A. Not usually. I will print some other artist's work, but I don't take other commissions. They all seem to be three times as much trouble as they are worth.

Demolition Man, 26x32 inches, silkscreen, by Clay Huffman. © 1982 Clay Huffman

In Chicago there is a group called the American Society of Artists, another kind of cooperative that accepts members from all over the country. They run a cooperative gallery in Chicago by paying people to sell the work, list their artists on a lecture service, and send mailings about their activities out on request.

Make a few inquiries in your area and you will find your niche. There are smaller, less formidable cooperatives, too. Many small art centers accept artists without any screening of their work. Try those first; then move on.

Gallery Sales

Gallery selling will probably contribute to part of your income, but some artists sell only through galleries and have their commissions handled only through them. The interview with Charles Pitcher is an example of an artist who makes most of his sales through galleries.

Charles Pitcher
Artist
Pittsburgh, Pennsylvania

Q. What kind of gallery connections do you have?
A. Right now, I'm under contract to one gallery in my home area. But I have two others in more distant towns.
Q. How many galleries do you think an artist should have to produce a decent income?
A. For me, it takes about three which are really working for me. If I get involved with a couple that do not sell as fast, then I would need about five galleries. In other words, three hard-working galleries or five

Triangles Three, 22x30 inches, watercolor, by Charles Pitcher.

slow-moving galleries. Each gallery should sell one painting per month on the average. I once went seven months without any income, but the galleries had all sold about double their average right before that. Then sales picked up again and I was back on an even keel. But those seven months were very hard to take. When something like that happens you wonder if you will ever make a sale again. Generally, the gallery sales average has stayed constant. An artist has to learn to live with things like that. It's frightening, but you have to keep the faith.

I keep about six paintings in each gallery at all times. In the out-of-town galleries, I change unsold paintings once a year. At home, I change two or three paintings every six weeks or so. Nothing is ever left for more than a year. Even that may be too long. It's a good idea to remove paintings often, so your public gets to know that they do not have forever to make up their minds to buy.

Q. Your galleries are all commercial, aren't they? Do you ever sell in cooperative space?

A. I used to sell in co-ops. They are cheaper. The commission is lower, but I feel that the people who run them don't always have the drive of the commercial galleries. Don't get me wrong, I'm not putting the co-ops down, but the gallery owner who knows he has to live by selling has more incentive. No matter how much effort the co-op people put in, they know they won't starve if they don't sell. Of course, if it's artists who are running the co-op, sometimes you get into other problems. I feel commercial galleries have produced better for me.

Q. What advice do you have for artists just starting out?

A. Establish a reputation in your own backyard. Professional shows, professional organizations, awards – do as much as you can. Get your name before the public. The people who buy art only know what they hear, see, or read. That's all. Visibility – that's the key. And take heart; it does work.

As you can see, you can have more than one gallery, but no more than one per small town. In large urban areas you might have several galleries; one, say in Bethesda, Maryland, and another in Alexandria, Virginia, all of which would be in the Washington, D.C. area, but widely separated. It depends on the requirements of your galleries. Some galleries consider a certain number of miles to be their area and request you to be exclusive with them in that area. Be sure you want to give them their demands before you join a gallery. Get a contract that spells everything out. Galleries usually provide these. (See Chapter 9 for information on how to protect your work, gallery bankruptcy, and copyright.)

Locating Galleries

When you feel it is time for you to exhibit out of town, how do you find a gallery? Write to them, of course. Buy copies of art magazines – the kind read by collectors as well as artists. Look at the gallery ads and review them for six months or so to find some that look as though your work would fit. Send letters and your biography, any good printed pieces about you, and slides of at least five paintings. Some galleries want a long track record, so don't be modest.

Be prepared to write many letters and to spend a good deal of time on this. Eventually, you may have enough responses to merit a trip to the new city to check out the galleries in person. More likely you will end up just sending work. In that case, be sure to send your work in such a way that you receive a signature of acceptance from someone at the gallery. Know where your paintings are at all times.

At the time this book was written, most galleries charge at least a 40 percent commission. Some galleries have gone as high as 60 percent. That's unfortunate; they do have a problem of survival, but the artist also suffers in giving up all that money, especially when the artist bears all the cost of framing and shipping. A good gallery should make contacts for the artist, have at least one or two one-person shows per year for the artist, pay at least half of the artist's reception costs, and sell at least three paintings per month. Sales galleries in smaller museums sometimes take only 20 percent commission. Many of the cooperative galleries also have low commission rates. Sometimes it is hard for artists not to feel that everyone is making money off our efforts. Try to grin and bear it. We need galleries, and until someone comes up with a better way to sell art, we must pay the price.

I have found a few of the smaller galleries that will buy my work outright. That helps because I don't have the suspense of waiting for a painting to sell. When you find a gallery that will do this, go for it! If your work sells higher than you expected, just charge more the next time. Be delighted it went that way, instead of the gallery being stuck with your unwanted work.

How does a gallery find an artist it wants to exhibit and what are some of the problems a gallery faces? This interview with Jane Haslem gives information from a gallery owner's point of view.

Jane Haslem
Owner
Jane Haslem Galleries
Washington, D.C.

Q. How do you find artists?
A. I have this nightmare of seeing the colleges and universities producing forty thousand new artists per year, and no place for these beginning artists to sell their work. I can't look at all the new artists' work. It's impossible.
Q. How does an artist get through the maze to have you look at his work?
A. It takes time. First, send three to five slides with a stamped, return envelope. Include a phone number. I don't want to see a résumé, don't

even read them. I just need to see the work first. Then, if I want more, I'll ask for it. Never drop in unannounced. I can answer only about five artists per week, even though I try very hard to keep up. Right now I'm eleven months behind in answers and the pile of slides grows each day. Extreme patience from the artist is required and no one feels worse about that than I do, but I'm doing the best I can.

Q. Do you have any more suggestions for the artists?

A. A business-like attitude is all I can suggest – and patience.

Q. Do you have any other ways of finding artists?

A. Yes, I jury shows and I check out university art departments. I'm always looking. But there are *so* many artists these days.

Q. How does the general art picture look to you?

A. These days people are spending money on necessities. We've got to find a way of countering that, and we gallery owners are trying. We are on the side of the artists, but we have so many pressures and, of course, our own budget problems. I wish we did not have to take 50 percent commission, but the artist has to realize it is hard to stay open as a gallery. Basics can cost as much as $5,000 per month; items like postage are a tremendous bill. I'm very much aware of artists' costs, but more aware of my own.

Presenting Your Work

After you have found a gallery of your choice, phone to make the appointment. Before your meeting, reorganize your portfolio of photos of paintings to gear it to this specific presentation. Take out any photos you think will not appeal to this particular gallery. Run through an imaginary presentation in your mind. Be prepared to answer all questions, preferably with some photos or printed material about yourself.

Use your small portfolio. Include photos of all of your paintings that fit the image of the gallery you are approaching. Take slides of other good works and your small viewer to show the slides properly. Be sure to have your printed résumé and a longer biography showing everything that you have done. Be prompt and organized. Keep your things conveniently packed so that you can find them quickly, making the presentation go smoothly.

Use psychology on yourself and the gallery director. Keep in mind how good you are – if there is interest in your work, your confidence will further impress the director. Don't rush, but don't waste the director's time. Take his lead. If he seems chatty, chat; but if he seems harried, get to the point. Be flexible. If some unforeseen emergency has entered his day, you might suggest that, if he wishes, you can come back. Of course, you mind doing this – but try to act as if his welfare comes first. It may swing the pendulum in your favor.

However, if the director seems disinterested in your work, then the gallery is probably not for you. It's hard to accept rejection kindly, but try. Getting upset or arguing with a gallery director only hurts you. Never try to justify or defend your work. Be positive. If it's no go, head for the next gallery. Rejections of an artist's work are not rejections of the artist, so don't take them personally. Keep in mind the good things that have happened to you.

When considering a gallery presentation, review Chapter 4. Also, read this interview with Komei Wachi, a gallery director in Georgetown, Washington, D.C. He knows his business well.

Komei Wachi
Director
Gallery K
Georgetown, Washington, D.C.

Q. How do you like an artist to present himself?
A. Don't bring artwork into the gallery. Bring slides or photos. I like your portfolio (gesturing to my small presentation portfolio described in Chapter 4), I wish every artist was prepared like this. It is good to see large color photos; slides are good, too. I need to see a résumé from the artist. When it is time to see the artwork, I generally request to go to the studio or ask for work to be brought in at that time. I like work tightly executed. I like realism with surrealism. It takes two or three years to get a show together. If you wonder about the pricing – $500 to $5,000 is the price range here. Higher takes doing.

Mr. Komei Wachi was very direct and pleasant and to the point. He answered almost everything I needed to know in one statement. Interviews like these are invaluable to you. It takes courage to arrange them, but you must do it. In the case of Mr. Wachi, I walked into the gallery one day and found him there. I asked if I could make an appointment to talk about my work and he agreed. Later I asked him a few more questions.

Q. What percentage does your gallery take?

A. That depends on circumstances. Some artists are very poor. We are very conservative; very much for the artist.

Q. Does the gallery do anything such as framing for the artist?

A. That depends, too, but generally I like ready-to-hang work.

Recording Consignments

The gallery will probably have a contract for you to sign. Your own consignment records can be made up on memos that you can buy in office supply stores. An example:

This is to certify that on __ (date) __ I left on consignment with __ (gallery name) __, __ (number) __ paintings to be sold with a __ (amount) __ percent commission of the retail price to be retained by the gallery.

List the title, medium, size, whether framed or unframed, and retail price for each painting. For example:

1. Fall Roses, watercolor, 22 x 30 inches framed; retail price $400.
2. Midnight Sun, acrylic on canvas, 24 x 44 inches framed; retail price $1,200.
3. Driftwood Bay, watercolor, 22 x 30 inches unframed; retail price $250.

Artist (signature) _____

Gallery Director (signature) _____

Address of gallery _____

Phone number of gallery _____

You can type these up a few at a time to save printing costs or they can be handwritten. Don't leave paintings without records. If you choose to use only the gallery's forms, that's okay. Don't forget, in your excitement about having your work shown, to get a *signature* on a receipt.

Buy a special notebook for recording sales and keeping other records on galleries. Paste your consignment slips in this book. Your sales slips go into your tax record book. Keep a record of sales in both the gallery notebook and the tax record book.

Gallery Checklist

Now that you are showing in galleries, review all the criteria for being professional. Be sure your framing is attractive and sturdy. Never take a painting out of a gallery in order to sell it to a client at a lower price, even if some buyers suggest it to you. This is one reason that galleries like to sell work from artists who live out of town. Be careful to keep your prices fairly consistent all across the country. If you sell in Chicago and also in Pittsburgh, or even in such widely separated cities as San Francisco and New York, you will be surprised at how often a person from one area will see your work in another. If they see it at a cheaper price than the one they paid, you may be in for trouble. It is important to figure your prices by some realistic method. Charge what you honestly feel the traffic will bear for your work, and stick to it. Go up gradually.

Checklist for exhibiting in galleries:

- Art magazines to locate galleries
- Brochure to send to galleries
- Portfolio to show galleries
- Color slides of your work and portable projector
- Plexiglas instead of glass on paintings
- Consignment record for gallery to sign
- Notebook to keep record of sales and consignments

After you become established with a gallery, you should constantly evaluate your performance as well as the gallery's. Are they selling for you? If a gallery is not generating at least one sale a month for me, I feel I'm not being properly represented. These sales can be averaged over several months to arrive at a fair number of paintings sold. If, for example, you had a one-person show and sold twelve paintings, then you could say the gallery was producing one sale per month for that year. Remember, if you don't keep the gallery supplied with enough work, you can't expect sales. It works both ways.

As a conclusion to this chapter, here are some anonymous comments from an artist who has tried the New York gallery scene for the past few years.

"It's tough here. It's not the place for beginners or those with low stamina. Art, at best, is hard work and in New York, it is doubly hard. The competition here is so fierce that it's frightening. The galleries are swamped with artists, trying to be discovered. Of course, if you are good enough, you will be discovered, but it takes time and tremendous effort."

Chapter Eight

Choosing a Life-Style

There are many career approaches open to an artist. Do you think you would like to sell your work through galleries? Or sit in an outdoor show and meet the public? Could you do that for a living? As we've seen, some artists make a substantial living that way. Or would you rather spend your life in academia? How about illustration? What does a commercial artist do? What other ways are there to make a living by wielding your brush?

Sometimes we ask ourselves, what does the world *want* from an artist? What does the world want from *me*? We try our best and still it doesn't seem to be enough. It's not that the effort isn't great enough, but that what we think is our best is not what the world appreciates. The world expects miracles. It expects us to be super-human. Okay – we are! Who else can go way beyond what ordinary mortals think and accomplish? Who else is able to reach into eternity and take out a piece of it to show to the world?

So, what are some of the life-styles open to artists and what *does* the world want from us? We can try to find out by research. In this chapter I interview more artists and art buyers so that you can benefit from their experiences.

The art buyers' interviews are with prototypes of persons you may have to deal with. You'll discover they need you as much as you need them. Remember that. It's hard to overcome shyness when you show your work. Whenever I make a new contact, I feel inadequate. But I'm usually surprised and delighted by the treatment I receive. You can go a long way toward success just by being pleasant. Never bore an art buyer by expounding on your work. If the work doesn't speak for itself, you've lost anyway. Do everything you can to be concise about your objectives and find the needs of your clients. Thinking this way will pay big dividends.

For my part, I wanted a traveling life-style, and I spent more than two years using my paint brush to support my wanderlust. I didn't have to stop my itinerant ways and settle down. Maybe I haven't yet – I may take off at any minute. I discovered an artist can pretty much write his own ticket. So my first "interview" in this chapter is with myself.

(Photo by Mary Ann Davis)

Edna Wagner Piersol
Artist
Destin, Florida

Q. Could I pack my studio into my little brown car and take off, hanging a painting out the window with a sign stating: "For Sale for Supper"?
A. Travel! The love of my life! For years I had used every available chance to take long or short trips, but there were never enough chances. Now I wanted to avoid being tied to one area by a job. There were states I hadn't seen, and countries beckoning. But, where to find the money to get to them?

I've always suspected you can make a living as an artist and live the kind of life you want without tying yourself to a nine-to-five job. Now I wanted to prove it.

Like most artists, I'd been "around" in the art world, paid my dues in various places: being a paste-up artist (before I married), then exhibiting in shows and "doing" the outdoor shows selling paintings – sometimes. But, never enough of anything to support myself as a painter. Now I wanted to face the world and make my talent pay off.

The first step was a drastic one. I brought back to my studio every painting that was out in a gallery unless it required shipping. Most of the pictures I took out of their frames for easier packing. Then I sorted them into categories of things that might sell in various parts of the country: pelicans for Florida; horses for Kentucky and Indiana; figure sketches for Pittsburgh and Cincinnati, for example.

After sorting, I took a hard look at my records. What kinds of outlets had produced good results over the last two years? I thought of hitting the outdoor show trail because I'd had some success at it, but I wanted a different, more businesslike approach. Also, I did not want to plan my itinerary around places and times when outdoor shows would be available.

Fortunately, I had built up a small clientele, decorating and frame shops, who would buy outright from me. That approach had paid off. A lot of money can be gambled on framing and show fees. At this time, I needed a surer thing.

My little list of clients had been gained casually by dropping in on shop owners and showing a few paintings. These clients were in towns along a route I often followed when visiting friends and relatives. How could I build on this list to extend it so I could go where I wanted all over the country – maybe the world?

I decided on a three-pronged attack: 1. small decorating and framing shops; 2. department stores; 3. large corporations.

Q. If I painted hard for two weeks out of every month, and then went on a selling trip, could I make a living?

A. I could keep myself in one place for two weeks by renting cheap vacation cottages out of season, and by staying with friends whenever possible. Now came some planning and figuring. When I thought about gallery sales I had to realize that if I sold a framed painting for $350, the gallery took 40 percent (some take even more). That left me with $210. The cost of producing a framed picture was at least $50, not to mention the shipping costs. I was left with $160 at most.

I was sure I could sell the same picture, unframed, for $160. So, what would I be losing? When traveling this way, gas, food, and lodging are *all* tax deductible. It seemed worth a try. If it worked, I'd be

Death & Resurrection, 36x28 inches, watercolor, by Edna Wagner Piersol.

going where I wanted to go, on one long "vacation," and deducting all my expenses.

I put together a presentation portfolio. I kept up with my expenses by calling people who had expressed interest in my work, making small, quick sales as I went. I found a certain amount of work produced a certain amount of money.

When I felt ready, I headed for Indianapolis because it was a big city, yet small enough not be be too frightening. I arrived with just enough money for one night in a motel, food for one day, and a gasoline credit card. I had to sell.

In the Yellow Pages I found ads for two large department stores, and two or three ads for interior decorators and frame shops. Sometimes the latter buy original work and sometimes not. My phone calls were short and businesslike. I've found you should not put yourself into a subordinate position; you must be sure of yourself, so you are tactfully interviewing your prospective client. Find out if he buys art directly from an artist and if he sounds good for you. If he doesn't, then don't waste time! When a call goes sour, just scan the Yellow Pages for the next prospect.

From my calls I lined up two appointments for the next morning and two for the afternoon: a frame shop and a department store in the morning; decorators for the afternoon. (Decorators are hard to find in the morning; they are usually visiting clients.) My approach to frame shops and department stores is similar. First, phone for an appointment. The person you need to see is the buyer, who is usually located in the picture and mirror department. Don't be discouraged if, after an appointment is made, it takes awhile to see him. Buyers are often busy and can't avoid being called out of their offices. Be patient and ready with your samples and wares. Make the most of your few minutes and be enthusiastic!

Just as with the phone calls, I try to do the interviewing. I stay pleasant, polite, and smiling, but I firmly decide if my work is right for this place. I stop wasting time as soon as I feel the buyer is not enthusiastic. I don't take offense if he's not interested.

By the end of my first day in Indianapolis, I'd made enough sales to assure my stay in town through the "Indy 500" (about a week). But, don't think it's always that easy. All calls do not produce sales. My average is one sale out of every three or four contacts. In Indianapolis I landed two big clients: a large department store and the biggest decorator in the area.

My courage was growing. I wanted to head still further from home – all those unvisited states and far countries were still calling me – but I felt the need to go to a place where I'd been before. I wanted to revisit Maine. But money was an issue again; how would I get there?

Maybe it was time for a big presentation to a corporation. I had the picture for it, a painting that had been too successful to sell unframed. It had been in several good shows, and I'd used it on my invitations and brochures. I knew the corporation collection I'd like it to be in. A telephone call to the art buyer for the corporation was politely received and an appointment was made. I told him the truth as enthusiastically as possible – that I had my most successful painting in town with me and, until now, had not been anxious to sell it. I explained that I was ready to have it become part of a good collection. Within a week my painting was sold and now belongs to the corporation. Success – and more courage.

Up to this point I had been living from day to day. This large sale turned me into a prudent soul again. I felt the urge to put most of the money in a bank against the day when I might need to pay my hospitalization or something similar. So I did, but I also called a friend in Maine and said I would be up to visit. By now I was confident I'd get money from somewhere. It sounds great to have friends to visit, but you must remember that there are gas, motels, and food to be paid for on the way. (I always think I'll eat "cheap" by going into grocery stores and buying inexpensive lunch meat and cheese. But I've been shocked into realizing that there is no such thing as cheap lunch meat and cheese.)

There was still another way of making money I had not yet explored. Several people wanted me to teach classes. A few phone calls told me I could hastily put together a small workshop. There wouldn't be many students, but there would be enough tuition to assure my being able to travel to the next place when I was ready.

A small group suited me fine for the Maine workshop. One student wanted to ride with me in my car and share expenses. Great! In my new life-style I don't have to do things "big"; all I need is enough to meet expenses.

The rest of my trip to Maine was financed by a student who didn't go along. Instead, she bought two paintings from me when I informed her of the workshop plans. Talking and telling people about what I was doing proved to be a big asset. Sometimes we are too quiet about our hopes. My sales have been going well because I say that I want to sell, and I keep my prices reasonable.

I certainly don't give my work away, although I've done some bartering. I've traded a painting for work on my car, and one for a place to stay the night – for legal advice and dental work, too.

Some artists would say my methods are not for them. They feel they must be producing for museums, winning awards. Fine . . . let them go to it! My chance for fame may or may not come, but in the meantime, I want to live! I keep my painting standards high! Sometimes I win awards with one painting from a series I originally did to sell to decorating shops. Never do I palm off on a gullible buyer something I don't feel is good work. Frankly, my buyers are getting bargains. They know it and I know it, but I'm not starving. The learning experiences in my new life are rewarding. Supposedly, you can't teach an old dog new tricks, but I'm discovering a whole new world! Many artists of the past made their day-to-day living just as I'm trying to do.

In Maine I never passed up an opportunity to sell. One morning I went to the beach to paint, and a woman came up to watch me. After a few minutes she told me that the gift shop at Fifth and Main would be interested in my work. I used to just thank people for this kind of information and say I'd check it out later. Not anymore!

When someone gives me information on prospective clients, I take time to talk to this person as I did with the woman on the beach. How reliable was she? What was her purpose in telling me about the shop? You'll probably find out a lot if you ask her if you can use her name when calling on the new client. The shop *was* interested – $300 worth of sales!

When the Maine interlude was over I headed for Washington, D.C., where my mail caught up with me. There were two letters from far-away cities, both unvisited places, and both gave promise of future work. Living by my paint brush is fun!

Q. Will I do this forever?

A. I don't know.

Ed Reep
Artist-in-Residence
Professor of Painting
East Carolina University
Greenville, North Carolina

Q. You are the author of *The Content of Watercolor*, and you teach painting at East Carolina University. How would you describe your life?

A. A good life, working in an environment where I feel needed and productive. For the most part, I have a rather simple routine; I teach in the mornings and paint in the afternoons, and sometimes evenings and weekends, if I wish. Evenings and weekends, however, more often than not, are devoted in part to writing and university obligations. It is surprising how much can be accomplished by working steadily throughout the year. And for exercise I play golf.

Q. What do you consider your most important accomplishments as an artist?

A. I have survived and raised a fine family – all intelligent, good citizens, and all have had the benefits of a fine education. Being an artist in our society is difficult. Unscrupulous businessmen can prosper; artists, musicians, dancers, actors – creative persons – can't hide their levels of inadequacy for the most part. But I can't complain. It is disconcerting to think that as a young artist, specifically a World War II artist/correspondent, I performed dutifully to the extent that I may be remembered more for that work than any other. For those who know me and my later efforts, I am considered a damn good teacher who has produced, and continues to produce, some good paintings and expressive drawings.

I write and have recently added two chapters to my book, which is scheduled to be republished in the fall of 1983 as a revised and updated edition. I am at work on another book, one that's not devoted exclusively to art. The most important contribution that my book on watercolor made was to underscore the fact that a fine watercolor is as important as a fine oil. For years, watercolor had been relegated to a second class status.

Q. Did you ever work at anything that didn't involve art? If so, how did you feel about that?

A. I worked at everything and anything to get through art school, which was a long, five-year, sleepless grind of night, day, and weekend work. I was a child of the Great Depression, and jobs were scarce – rare. But every job I've had since those days, including the last four years of army service, has been art related: mural painting, commercial art, motion picture designing, illustration, scenic painting, teaching, and always, easel painting. All the while I continued to exhibit, write and lecture. I would rather see a budding, young artist sweep floors and paint what he must, than to prostitute his efforts. I don't consider commercial work, bona-fide commissions, and assignments to be out of order. I do feel sorry for those who do not produce the good effort, or who knowingly pander second-class work, even to survive, for they are soon reduced to that level.

Q. How do you feel about teaching as a creative part of your life? Is it as rewarding as painting?

A. I have *made* teaching a creative part of my life to the best of my ability. Obviously, teaching has been a necessity for my survival and I am grateful to be able to do it for that reason. It has allowed me to do what I wish without compromising standards or directions. But there are times when teaching can be enervating and distracting despite the rewards, such as the dialogue with colleagues and good students, feedback of ideas, the development and guidance of young people, and personal pride in doing a good job. Starting students in valid directions – teaching them how to become *learners* and how to continue their lifelong studies – that's the rub.

As to the second part of your question, we can no more compare the rewards of teaching to those of painting than we can compare apples to oranges. Each has separate qualities, separate reasons for existing.

Q. What advice would you give to painting students about making a living as an artist?

105

A. I tell all of my students that it would be a miracle if they could survive on painting sales alone, unless they are geniuses and so recognized. Most artists who make it to the top are good, but they are also very clever and conscious of public relations. They seem possessed with enormous drive, are ego-oriented and ambitious. It is a fact of life that many who wish to be well-known, famous, or to see their works in museums throughout the world, just won't, or can't, pay that heavy a price. This is assuming that their work merits such acceptance.

Since I have never been able to subsist on painting sales alone, I offer students careful advice. Weigh all consequences, explore other avenues of income that afford free time to paint, find out who you are and how you are constituted – what your needs and desires are. What are you willing to sacrifice to attain life goals?

(The author disagrees with this answer, but it must be noted that Mr. Reep's opinion fairly represents that of many artist/teachers.)

Ode to Antonio Gaudi, 29x35 inches, collage, by Ed Reep.

Untitled, 60x60 inches, oil on canvas, by Ed Reep.

Jerry Caplan
Professor of Art
Chatham College
Pittsburgh, Pennsylvania

Q. You've won many awards in both painting and sculpture. You've had one-person shows and sold work that way for years. I know that you are an innovator in clay and have developed the Pipe Sculpture Workshops in Ohio, Pennsylvania and California, using factory facilities. Do you think of yourself as a professor of art or an artist?

A. I consider myself, or at least hope I might be, a proto-type – artist-teacher. It's not an easy job to teach. One must love and need to teach. However, if you never do anything else but teach, you have nothing on which to draw. A young teacher teaches by facts, an older teacher has a reservoir of information.

Q. What was your first job?

A. My very first job was with my Dad in his wholesale produce market. He wanted me to follow the family tradition. I did freelance commercial art and department store display, photographed parties, painted signs, and designed posters; but when I got a job in a clay factory it turned my whole life around. That's where I first met "the cylinder" and became fascinated with it. The cylinder is still very prominent in my work. It serves as both the armature and the skin of the sculpture. I've never tired of it.

Q. So you've never really worked at anything noncreative?

A. Not really, now that I think of it. Another early job was making mannequins. It seems I was always drawn to jobs that required work with my hands. I guess I've always lived by art.

Q. Did you ever have any times when you didn't know if you could make a living?

A. Oh, sure! Everyone goes through those times. It was back when my wife and I were first married. We were living in New York and it was then that our first son came along. We wanted to move to a better place to bring him up. We wrote letters everywhere, all over the country. The local art guild of a southern town responded. They offered to help us start a school. They located space; we arrived and fixed it all up. Then the leadership of the guild changed, some of the support fell through, and well, we were on our way. We really struggled, but we made it for a while. It was during that time that I painted my first mural; got paid by the square yard. I accepted all jobs in those days. I

Undulating Dome, glazed stoneware, by Jerry Caplan.

remember that I was paid $1,500 for that mural because I went right out and bought a shiny, taffy apple, wooden-body station wagon. It was wonderful to look out the window and see that car out there.

Q. You have made some discoveries. If you were a scientist, you'd be in research?

A. Yes, could be. Part of creativity is innovation: discovering new techniques, combining unusual materials, finding new applications. For instance, I've found a new way to use Raku that utilizes no glaze, but results in a drawing made with smoke.

Q. Let's get back to the clay factory. You made sewer pipe, did you not?

A. No. I counted how many pipes were made every ten minutes. To keep from falling asleep, I took some pipes off the line and started carving them. Discovering how to make sculpture from sewer pipe had a profound effect on my work. Now I know the power of the cylinder. I've used it both geometrically and biomorphically.

Q. Sensuality seems to be a recurring theme in your work. Why?

A. While I do other subjects, the female form is an important preoccupation. It has been the symbol of love and beauty for many centuries; not only sex. Women represent togetherness, separation, abundance. They are the vessel of civilization.

Q. Togetherness and separation at the same time?

A. I guess it is the relationship between man and woman; one needs the other, two forms interdependent but independent, each having its own identity.

Q. You do both painting and sculpture. Which is the real you?

A. I'd rather be called an artist than either painter or sculptor. For a long time I thought I had to choose, but that's not true. They work themselves out. I feel strong in each direction. Sometimes I'll do sculpture for a whole year, then because of some catalyst, switch around and turn to painting. I'm an *artist* who is creating; that's what it's all about. I've always refused to work at anything else.

Q. What advice would you give a young artist who wanted to be "just like you"?

A. Start early, teach when you have something to pass along and want to help someone else grow, but *live*, too. Of course, you must have credentials to teach on the college level, so quite a bit of schooling goes into the living. Be an artist first; be sensitive to relationships, think creatively, and enjoy the act of making art.

Charles Beacham
Commercial Artist
Watercolorist
Pittsburgh, Pennsylvania

Charles Beacham is a commercial artist with Creamer Associates and art director for the Arts and Crafts Center of Pittsburgh, in addition to being a watercolorist and art teacher.

Q. What is the most important thought you could pass on to an aspiring artist?

A. I believe it is important that we learn to accept the quality about each of us that is unique. How do I see life? What do I think about it? It is only by self-expression or intuition that our paintings take on a unique sensitivity. As a man thinks in his heart, etc.; that is the truth we are all trying to express, and that is what gives your paintings a soul and a life of their own. In other words, be sincere, do your own thing, and have fun.

Q. I remember so well a day when I was studying in your class, and another student asked you when you were going to teach us how to paint a tree. You said, "My God! Why would I do that?" Do you remember the rest of your answer that day?

A. [Chuckle] I do. "How do you think that a tree looks? You don't learn to paint a tree. You *feel* a tree. You are not a camera. Painting follows feeling. You learn to paint, period. You learn to apply pigment to paper, then you learn to feel your subjects. Then you put them onto paper."

Q. What was your first job?

A. I went directly from school to an art director's job. It was really bad for me. I had no idea how art was made. How could I direct art without knowing how it was reproduced? So, by my own doing, I went back, or I should say into (since I had never been there before) being an artist in a studio – to learn the fundamentals.

Q. How in the world did you get an art director's job right out of school?

A. Well, I worked nights in the supply room at school to help pay my tuition, and one night, when no one else was around, a phone call came in from a new agency – I guess they were as inexperienced as I – and they asked if we had anyone qualified to be an art director. I said, "You bet." I asked when I could interview, went the next day, and conned my way in. But I soon realized the folly of trying to do a job one is not prepared to do.

Q. Then how did you finally get into fine art?

A. After a good many years of commercial art, I took a class in watercolor for fun. Then I began to enter shows and to win awards and some recognition. Soon I was teaching watercolor at the art center. That is the way it has gone on.

Q. Did you ever think you could quit the commercial work to devote full time to painting?

A. No, I was always afraid to do that. Wish I had your advice back then. Now, I *might* try it.

Fantasy, 28x36 inches, watercolor, by Charles Beacham.

Claire Justine
Artist
Marathon, Texas

Q. You have exhibited and sold in the United States and Europe, and made your living for years by painting. What is your approach to selling your work?
A. Alternative spaces and sales (those that do not involve galleries) are a godsend for the artist. Most often, gallery sales can be slow, especially on major pieces, or when the artist is first establishing a reputation. When you are trying to earn a living, checks from galleries can seem to be far apart from each other.
Q. How did you arrive at that approach?
A. I opened a studio in 1977 in the downtown area of Louisville, Kentucky. I was determined to have my art pay the way. I was still teaching one class a week, giving several private lessons a month, judging an occasional exhibit, and holding infrequent workshops. But this wasn't getting my art in front of the public. I had lots of ideas and I felt it was a good time to try them.

For years I had been painting watercolor cards for family and friends to send on various occasions and holidays. I decided to turn this into a profitable sideline. My first contact was a small card shop on the first floor of the same building as my studio. It had just opened and the owner had admired some of the hand-painted cards I had shown her, so I asked if she would like to carry some in her shop. She was delighted. My cards, which had messages inside, sold almost immediately and more were ordered. The favorite was one with

113

several strawberries on the front and the inside message of "I wish you strawberry days and whipped cream nights." By the time I received my third order in as many weeks, the owner and I had agreed on a wholesale price and a minimum amount of cards per order. The name I selected for my card venture was Very Personal Greetings and I was in business for real!

I followed the sale of the cards by approaching other shops. The owner of the first shop requested that I set up a place to paint in her shop on a Saturday before such occasions as St. Valentine's Day and Mother's Day. This was good advertising for both of us. The cards were more than just a greeting, but not quite a gift, and they were suitable for framing – a point I used in my own advertising.

Once the card business got going, I began to do small watercolor florals painted on silk, matted and mounted in narrow gold or silver frames. These I marketed to small gift and museum shops. In marketing work like this, the artist must be aware these paintings are gift items and should be priced accordingly. Keep in mind that the shop owner must have at least a 50 percent markup.

The money coming in from this and my other art related ventures was enough to pay for the rent on my studio, my supplies, and give me

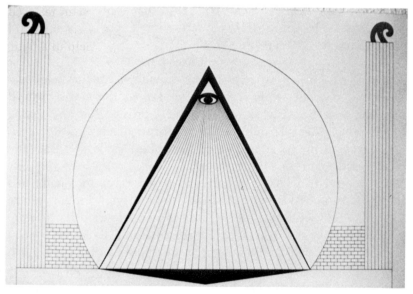

The God's Eye, 22x30 inches, pen and ink, by Claire Justine.

a small profit. I was still selling major work out of my studio, which was open to the public from eleven to five, Tuesday through Saturday.

After a year, five shops were carrying my cards as well as two museum shops and several shops and galleries in some small towns nearby. When I remarried and moved to El Paso, Texas, halfway across the country, I began again and, within two months, had three shops carrying the cards and two carrying the small watercolor paintings on silk. Within another three months, I had four more shops in four resort towns as well as a good gallery in a major tourist center.

Later I started my own gallery in a facility that was open only on weekends and catered to the tourist trade. It was an indoor market place for small businesses featuring arts and crafts, and was a huge success. I carried my major paintings as well as the cards, small paintings on silk, some of my own posters and, at Christmastime, some handmade ornaments. My shop was in the gallery listings in the Sunday paper. I changed the major paintings every month. One month I would feature watercolors, another month, acrylics, and another, pen and ink. In October I featured autumn leaves done in watercolor on silk, and in November and December, small gift paintings that were relatively inexpensive.

An additional touch my customers came to enjoy was a newsletter called *Comments from Claire's Corner* which focused on the featured paintings of that month, maybe a new card design, an activity that I was involved in that was newsworthy, and always a helpful artistic hint.

It was a successful venture, artistically and financially. So much so that recently, my husband, who is also an artist, and I have moved back to my family's ranch north of Marathon, Texas. I'm writing again – some art books and a return to poetry – something I did even before painting. Am I painting? Oh, yes, more than ever, and thoroughly enjoying the quiet life with no phone or TV and only marginal radio reception. I'm also hoping to begin work on my master's degree in art.

Steve Gentile
President, Gentile Brothers
Screen Printing
Arlington, Virginia

Q. Your corporation has grown from a one-man business to what it is today by hard work and determination. What brought you to this way of making a living?

A. I always knew that I wanted to be an artist. I decided at eighteen to get into something where I could be creative. I had the urge to express myself through pretty things to look at – painting, sculpture. I tried several things. Architecture was what I chose first and I studied it for a little while. I excelled at the drawing but didn't like the physics and math. I played around at welding to learn metal sculpture and got a job making stairways. That's hardly an artist's position. I tried clay on a [potter's] wheel and liked that, but then I hit on printing and sign-making. And they worked for me. Neon sculpture has fascinated me since I first saw it, but I'm really not into that yet.

Q. So your only schooling in art was as a would-be architect?

A. Yes. Otherwise, I was self-taught in everything.

Q. Did you have any jobs that weren't connected with art?

A. Only the usual ones when I was very young; like paper boy, delivery boy. I once made meatballs in an Italian restaurant. Then I got my first art-connected job. I became a printing trainee in a sign shop. I did the hand-cut designs. My second sign shop job was as a printer – no longer a trainee. Then [I did] trade show stuff in the printing department of a display production company.

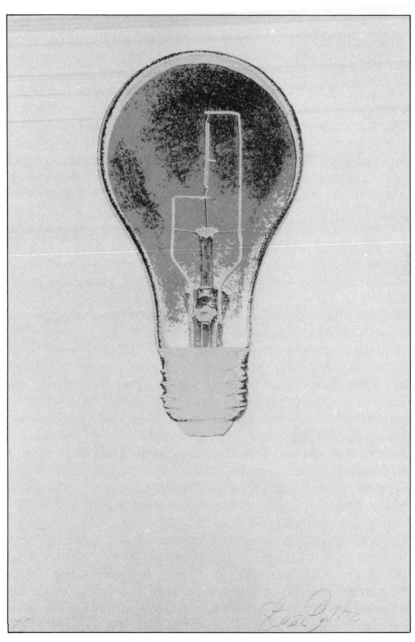

Light Bulb, 20x15 inches, screen print, by Steve Gentile.

Q. How did you finally get out on your own?

A. By keeping my eyes open. I wanted to be on my own, so I asked questions in order to be able to hurry and learn. You can either become an expert in a year or two, or you can take twenty years to do it. Applying yourself is the key. That determines whether it will take years to climb the ladder or whether rapid advancement is achieved.

Q. After you went out on your own, how long was it until you began to put a company together?

A. I was working at home in a basement workshop; my brother Dave worked at a photo job to support us while I managed the printing and organizing of the business. Soon we moved into a place zoned for industry and hired our first helper: a printer. We slowly added people one at a time; then, a few years ago, we decided to really expand. That was after Dave took a tour of Europe to see how experts over there did things. We decided to specialize. We realized we needed to be equipped to do a few things well, really well. That is the key to success.

Q. Do you feel that you have deserted your first love of being an artist by going into the commercial end of the business?

A. Not at all. I have sold some paintings, but I was discouraged by the gallery scene. I soon abandoned all the stuff you'd have to go through to get into that. And my dreams for the future hold an art print division for Gentile Brothers. I hope someday "Gentile Atelier" (dealing exclusively with fine artists) will come into existence. There are wonderful ways to use screen printing, like making twenty-color or fifty-color editions. Someone in Europe does hundreds of colors. Of course, that's an obsession, but it's interesting. There are ways of reproducing a painting by almost "painting" it over with screen printing runs. It creates a beautiful picture that is nothing like ordinary reproduction methods.

Q. How much would the artist who painted the picture be involved in that?

A. Very much. The artist could make the hand-painted color separations. The other method is to have another person do the separations. Either way, the result is tremendous in terms of producing beautiful work.

Q. How can other aspiring artists benefit from what you have learned?

A. Well, I'd say that applying yourself is the key. Decide what you want to do and set out to do it.

Jane Paleceh
Art Director
National Wildlife *Magazine*
Vienna, Virginia

Q. How do you like being an art director?

A. I love it. I create with type and layout rather than a brush, but I just love it.

Q. How did you get where you are?

A. Well, I got a bachelor of arts degree from Cardinal Stritch College in Milwaukee, Wisconsin. I was trained to be a teacher and then there were no jobs. I became an apprentice in an ad agency, learned production, paste-up, etc., and did some illustrating. In agencies, you don't move up from within. I was underpaid for three years, then I moved on. I got a job as a designer at Golden Books. They were in Racine, Wisconsin then; now they are in New York. After that I became an art director at Raintree Publishers Group in Milwaukee and was there for six years, and now I'm at *National Wildlife* as art director. I came here because I wanted to work on a magazine, one that has moral value.

Q. You buy work produced by illustrators, do you not?

A. Yes. And at one time I painted a lot, myself, and did illustrating.

Q. What do you expect from an artist who wants to illustrate for your magazine?

A. Be realistic about your talents. It's important to find a mentor to criticize your work and to *listen* to that mentor. So many would-be illustrators come in, saying, "This is my portfolio," and the stuff is dreadful. Artists don't try hard enough to find out what is wanted. I always know when I'm meeting a "dead ender" because that artist gets hostile when hearing constructive criticism. That's so unnecessary. There is never just one way of solving a problem. Give and take is better. Talk to the art director and find out what is wanted. Maybe the art director will like your idea if it is explained, but if he doesn't, don't argue. Tantrums are not accepted, being reasonable is.

Q. When you choose an illustrator for a certain job, how much leeway do you give?

A. I'm very specific. I give a layout and definite instructions. For instance, I might say I want a scratch board illustration, or I'll request a pen-and-ink or watercolor rendering. The illustrator knows exactly what I want before leaving with the assignment.

Q. Is there anything else you want to say to artists?

A. Yes, one thing should be said loud and clear and it is a "don't do." *Don't* send samples of your work with a letter saying, "I'd like to publish these. Please let me know how soon you can do it." You'd be surprised how many times I get that kind of thing. My comment always is, "Are they from another planet or something?" I know they are going to be hard to work with. Even if the artwork is fantastic, I'd never use it. They have personality problems that no one needs.

Q. What makes a good illustrator?

A. Good basic drawing for one thing. Most artists don't work hard enough at that. In fact, being an artist is tough! It takes hard work.

Q. What else would you say it takes besides good drawing and hard work?

A. Knowing color and composition, and the mechanical process of printing. Staying aware of new trends in illustration; using books like the *Illustrator's Annual* and *Art Director's Annual* to keep up with the market.

Joan Coate Milsom
Corporate Art Buyer, Artist
Pittsburgh, Pennsylvania

Q. You are a fine artist, and I know that you took this job as a corporate art buyer to expand your knowledge of painting, rather than to desert any part of your existence as an artist. How is it working? What are you learning that might benefit your fellow artists?
A. I've been an artist for as long as I have "been." By that I mean that I've always thought and felt color, and have been aware of the design and textures of all things around me. Most artists seem to live in this same world.

When you, as an artist, look at a piece of art that is not your own, you judge that work on its own merit. The artist's name is unimportant. That single visual interpretation is all that counts. Creative people are interested in studying other creations for stimulation and interest in new ideas. Each artist has an image of a successful creative unit that he applies to his own and others' work. If a piece doesn't measure up to your particular standards, it's a failure. I was surprised to find that this insider's view, of art for art's sake, is not necessarily shared by the purchasers of art.

When first offered the opportunity to buy art for a corporation, the prospect of reviewing thousands of works by accomplished and recognized artists, delighted me. But I soon found that the principles of buying art as an investment are contrary to the value judgments to which artists inside the art world adhere.
Q. By investment, what do you mean?
A. I do not mean buying masterpieces or artists' works that are hanging in museums. Instead, the art which *most* corporations buy

Jerusalem-The Old City, 68½x50½ inches, oil, by Joan Coate Milsom.
Collection of U.S. Bank, Portland, Oregon.

must act as decoration with investment as a secondary thought – an enhancing of the surroundings with, maybe, the potential to grow in value. The artwork must be in step with the corporation's image, keeping in mind that each corporation has its own personality. Therefore, I find myself looking at art in a new light. I had to examine the collective work of an artist to find consistent quality and constant progression. The idea is to buy work that will maintain or increase in value and still fit a particular corporate image.

Q. Are you glad that you have taken on the challenge of purchasing other artists' works for a corporation?

A. I think so. Buying corporate art broadens one's horizons since it forces one to look, to study, and to critique hundreds of works. I look for continuity – professionalism and the going value placed on each of the individual portfolios.

Buying artwork for a corporation has the usual frustrations for an artist. A tight budget and overexposure to too many works of art or too many styles bring on a severe case of creative overload. This results in loss of personal production time while trying to clear your saturated brain.

One day you are on the inside, creating and working hard; the next day, you are on the outside, looking in. Having lived on both sides of this coin, my desires are reaffirmed with each trip. I know that I must create. There is no other way, for me, to survive.

William Ackley
Art Director
Former Corporate Collection
Curator
Mellon Bank
Pittsburgh, Pennsylvania

Q. As curator, what types of paintings did you acquire for the corporate collection?

A. At Mellon Bank, they don't want nudes, or anything like that, so, as curator, I had to know the tastes of the clientele for whom I was working. I bought whatever fit into the criteria. I don't know how many paintings it has by now, but it must be six to eight thousand. And they all fit into this same criteria – no nudes and nothing pornographic. Usually nothing even impressionistic – all realism.

Q. Another kind of corporation might like something different, right?

A. Right, but in this particular institution, that's what is wanted and that's all we have.

Q. How would an artist have made you, as curator, aware of his work?

A. I usually hit all the galleries. And for years, we invited our own one-person shows and bought work out of them. The bank wants to stay local – buy local art.

Q. Would you say most corporations are like that?

A. No, I wouldn't. Large corporations go everywhere to buy.

Q. Would it hurt for an artist to call a corporate curator to try to make a sale?

A. Oh, no. It would be all right. An artist can call the corporation and ask who buys the art and then try to make an appointment.

Q. What kind of credentials would you want an artist to have before calling you?

A. I'd say he'd need something indicating that he'd sold else-where – and not just two paintings. However, if everything went right and he had painted just two paintings and they were good, I'd buy them.

Q. You know, Van Gogh sold very few paintings. Too bad he didn't live around you. I'm sure you would have bought some from him.

A. [Chuckle] Sure would. To tell you the truth, I don't think any modern Van Goghs go unnoticed these days. Galleries have sprung up all over the place. We've more galleries now than we know what to do with. It takes a lot of time to keep up with them all, but after a while you get to know where you want to go. You don't bother going some places. Their work doesn't fit here; it's for other clients.

Q. Are there many artists, do you think, who don't use galleries?

A. No. They [the artists] don't have time to go out and sell their work. I know that sometimes the price gets out of hand, but I think artists need galleries.

Q. Do you have any guide for artists who want to sell their work?

A. Price doesn't matter – not in this institution. The quality of work matters. Basically, this bank is looking for fine art with good decorative qualities and they pay the price for it. They want something to decorate the buildings.

Q. Do other banks feel this way?

A. I don't think so – look at this book from the Bank of Chicago.

Q. It's beautiful. Their collection is different from yours, is it not?

A. Yes, they seem to be setting themselves up as a collector of already established artists. We aren't. We like to encourage artists all through their careers.

It seems that choosing the life-style you want and then beginning to pursue it from your own backyard is the best step. Choosing is the most important factor. Decide where you want to live and how – and the rest will follow.

Chapter Nine

Business Sense

The minute you sell a painting, you are a business person, whether you like it or not. The more businesslike you are, the more profit you'll make.

There are pitfalls in the business of being an artist. One of them is that you must trust your work to others so often. What happens if a gallery goes bankrupt after you have consigned your work there? It depends on the laws of the state where you are living and working. It is entirely possible, unless you take precautions and get signatures on various legal forms before leaving your work, you could *lose* your paintings in the event the gallery goes into bankruptcy. It sounds unfair, and it is. Bankruptcy laws in some states are unclear, so be forewarned. Artists' Equity Association (Suite 1003, 1725 K St. NW, Washington, D.C. 20006) has information about this and many other problems, and is a good organization to join. As an artist on your own, you need all the information you can find to keep your work safe.

At this writing, very few states exempt artists from the laws governing consigned goods. Bankruptcy laws are designed to protect creditors, and consigned property is usually judged to be an asset of the bankrupt gallery, even though it is still owned by the artist. In some states, such as Florida, a form can be obtained from the Secretary of State of Florida which, if signed *before* consigning your work to the gallery, assures that your work will not be classified as part of the gallery's assets.

It is a good policy to review your records each month and remove gallery paintings and replace them with new ones every sixty days or so. That keeps you in touch with the gallery, and gives you a feeling for what is happening. If no paintings have been sold in sixty days, it is likely the gallery is not going to produce well anyway. At that time, give them a reason why you want to take all of your work out temporarily, and later you can return the paintings or submit new ones. It is a good plan to keep the inventory of paintings in the gallery low until you feel good about the establishment. Why take unnecessary risks?

Copyright

Copyright laws are another area that you should explore and get to know well. Today, the copyright laws in the United States state that the copyright of a painting belongs to the artist who produced it from the moment of its creation, unless the artist *signs* away his copyright. (A copyright can only be transferred in writing.) In other words, as long as an artist does not sell the copyright along with the work, the right to make money by reproducing it or by selling the reproduction rights to it belongs to the artist.

It is always a good idea to place your copyright notice (a c with a circle around it © followed by the year date and your name or an abbreviation by which your name can be recognized) on your paintings and slides, even though you have not yet offically registered your copyright with the copyright office. Official registration need not take place until an actual infringement of your copyright takes place; however, to be eligible to collect attorney fees and statutory damages (to be compensated for the infringement) the registration must occur within three months of the painting's publication. To further understand copyright, write or call the U.S. Copyright Office (U.S. Copyright Office, Library of Congress, Washington, D.C. 20559, 202-287-8700) and obtain the free Copyright Information Kit. Books on copyright are also available at your library.

Pricing Savvy

What to charge for work is always a puzzle. I can't count the times a student has asked me that question. The answer is that one artist's worth does not depend on that of any other artist. The price of your paintings is determined by the quality of your work and the strength of your name. Since the general public has a hard time believing in its own judgment, the strength of your name is important. Start out by noting what other artists are charging for comparable work. Check outdoor shows and galleries that carry new names. Set your prices accordingly. From then on, try whatever price the market will bear. If you are not getting as much money per painting as you think you should, look for reasons other than price. Maybe you are not in your right market. Another gallery or art center may be better for you. Never lower a price if you can avoid it. If you *must* do it, do it in a way that will not become common knowledge. For instance, tell the person in charge of sales that it will be all right to sell your paintings at X number of dollars less than the marked price, provided it is done quietly. That way, the public will have your original price as an example of the quality of your work.

As I mentioned earlier, never, under any circumstances, take a painting out of the gallery or show in order to sell it cheaper to a client. Sometimes an opportunistic buyer will suggest that you do this and split the gallery commission with him. Don't. Always discuss your sales with the gallery or show chairman and always pay the commission. You need the goodwill of those agents who sell for you.

There is a marketing rule about pricing that you can use as a guideline: The wholesaler doubles the manufacturer's price; the retailer doubles the wholesale price. In this case, you are both manufacturer and wholesaler. Let's say it cost you $50 to produce a painting in actual cost of materials. So you could let a gallery buy it from you, if they will, for $100; then they can sell it for $200.

If you sell a painting outright to a gallery, you lose all control over the final price. If the gallery can sell it for $300 instead of $200, they have the right to keep the extra money. Yet, that can work to the artist's advantage in terms of cash flow. When I need money, I often make an offer to a gallery or decorator, which enables them to buy two or more paintings at a reduced rate, with the stipulation that they must be sold at my regular retail price. This deal keeps my public price up, keeps the gallery happy, and gives me the money I need, instead of waiting for the paintings to sell to receive payment.

Usually a gallery won't buy outright, but will want to take a painting on consignment and make only a 40 percent commission. Then you will get $120 (if it sells at $200) instead of the $100.

If you prefer to judge the final price of your paintings by an hourly pay scale, figure the hourly rate you want. Add it, multiplied by the hours you have worked on the painting, to the cost of materials.

Example: You want to work at $10 per hour. You've worked five hours on the painting – the materials cost $50. You will want to wholesale the painting for $100.

It might be helpful to use an estimating form, like the one that follows, to help you gauge your pricing when you are talking to a prospective buyer about a commission. Do not give a price off the top of your head. Instead, find out what the client wants: size, type of pigment, and the time limits placed on you. Go back to your studio and figure out the cost of the commission in an organized way. Then give the client a solid price, based on cost and your markup for time. We artists are not very realistic creatures, so it is good to have a few forms to fill out in order to make our heads control our imaginations.

A sample estimation for a commission:

Materials and Time		Cost
1. Paper, canvas or other support (add in an extra piece for the failures)		$ 10.50
2. Colors	3 tubes at $.60	
	3 tubes at $.95	4.65
3. Hours spent painting	5 at $10.00	50.00
4. Research hours	2 at $10.00	20.00
5. Research material	2 rolls film plus developing	18.00
6. Mat and frame materials	(list all here)	45.00
7. Matting and framing hours	2 hours at $10.00	20.00
8. Plexiglas	1 piece	23.00
9. Delivery charge (also include gas for research and parking fees, etc.)	$0.17 per mile (15 miles)	2.55
		$ 193.70
10. Add 100 percent profit (This is called a 50 percent markup)		193.70
		$ 387.40

Round off this price to your customer to $385 (it sounds better than $387). Or have the courage to go to $400. I would.

Bookkeeping Basics

Setting up your books as a business person is a must. If you have an accountant or one in the family, you are lucky. If not, my simple set of books should serve you for a long time. The main thing to remember is that you must keep detailed records of sales and expenses plus *proof* of these transactions. Get information from the Internal Revenue Service about what records you will need and start from there. (Consult your telephone book for the number and location of your nearest IRS office. Most IRS information is now handled by telephone or by mail.)

My "books" consist of inexpensive student composition books with wire binders. On the front I write "Tax Records – (Year)" in bold magic marker. Head the first page *January, (year)* for a written record of the sales for January. Make columns for date/amount/client/payment arrangement. On the second page I glue proof of those transactions, i.e., gallery slips, sales slips, check stubs, etc. Three or four pages are left blank for more sales slips. Then on page five or six, I write a record of expenses for January – date/amount/type of puchase/store, and any

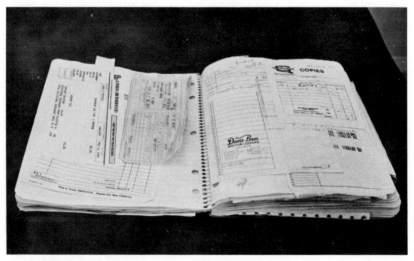

My tax record book. Notice how it keeps the proof of my transactions in one place, easily accessible, and organized by month. (Photo by Bob Young)

other pertinent data. On the following pages, I glue the sales slips and receipts that are proof of purchase.

The composition books are flexible enough to allow almost any expansion caused by the sales slips. No slip gets away as it might if you were sticking it into a folder. The last page for each month is a written recap of the month.

The only other records I keep are my check book and savings account book. When I make a deposit, I record in the bank book the name of the client from whom the payment came. If I need to transfer from one account to another, I make a note by the deposit: "from savings" or "from checking." Never make a deposit without some notation to show its source. Try to purchase everything, including supplies or even postage, by check. If you're forced to pay cash, make a note in your checkbook of the transacton. I make these notes on the date that a check would have been written. That way I never miss any expenses. The composition book records and sales slips serve as a backup.

Paying Yourself

Do you want the stability of a salary? It's fairly easy to set one up. First, face the fact that there will be long periods of time when you won't make money. Plan ahead. Start a "cash flow savings account," – one that has no penalty for withdrawals. (Consult your accountant, local savings and loan company, or bank.) You may have to draw out fairly large sums each time so as to avoid paying a penalty. (You can always put some back immediately.) Put every check or payment you receive into this cash flow account. Borrow to start the account if necessary. Simply pay yourself a certain set amount at the first of each month. You may have to do some budget revising in the beginning, but if you pare your living expenses down to a minimum and do a lot of planning about how you are going to make your money, you should have the hang of it in a month or two.

Now that I'm over the hump of adjusting to living as an artist, I have another way to set up my salary. These days I try to sell as many paintings as possible on time payments. If I get five or six payments of over $100 coming in per month, they go a long way toward meeting my expenses. Time payments without using a credit card give both you and your client an advantage. The client does not pay interest, which saves him a lot of money if he is paying for a $3,000 painting. The advantage for you is that you might not have made the sale otherwise, so what are you losing? Be careful though; once I almost lost the last $200 of an $1,800 sale because I forgot to get the client's signature. The buyer had paid me $1,600 and said he'd send the balance in a month. After six months my lawyer wrote him – fortunately this worked and he paid.

Set up your time payment sales the following way. On memo slips or sales slips from an office supply store, write the client's name and address, the item purchased, and details such as "unframed" or "as is" or "plus shipping." *Be sure you get the signature of the client on this.* Once that is done, you are pretty well protected.

If you do decide to make credit card sales available to clients, call one of the credit card company offices. (They're listed in the Yellow Pages.) They will send you information on becoming a member, so that people may charge their purchases with you on a credit card.

Benefits and Taxes

Since you will be working for yourself, you will have to supply your own health insurance and retirement fund. Don't neglect this. Include them in your budget for the year. Shop around for health insurance, and do check various art groups to see if an insurance plan is available for members. Talk to your bank and your insurance company about retirement options. Buy insurance immediately, at the earliest age possible, to get the best breaks. Whatever age you are, you'll never be any younger, so don't put it off.

When selling from your home studio, you will need a sales tax number, which also provides you with sales tax exemption on your art supplies. If you sell all of your work through galleries, you don't need to bother with it, unless you want the exemption on your supplies. Obtain tax information from your state tax office and the Internal Revenue Service and comply with it. You may also need a business license. Call your town's city hall to find out what's needed in the way of licenses or permits.

An accountant is invaluable at tax time. Your taxes as a self-employed business person are a little complicated, as you will see when you get your tax information. Your accountant isn't a miracle worker, so organize your information as well as you can for him. I never give mine the Tax Record composition book – that's my record. Instead I turn over to my accountant a neatly written single sheet of paper showing *all* of my expenses and sales for the year. The expenses must be broken down into certain categories. (Check with him in advance to see how he wants it done.) The categories may change from year to year, but a few to remember are: *Utilities* – if you use one room of a six-room house for studio space, you can deduct one-sixth of your utilities. Keep a separate list of utility charges. (If an artist wants to claim home office/studio space as a deduction, he must have a specific space that is used *regularly* and *exclusively* for his trade or business. It may be the artist's actual dwelling or a nearby separate structure used for business, but personal and business efforts must be kept separate.)

You can deduct *car expenses* by keeping track of mileage used for your business; a rate per mile is allowed. *Professional fees* – exhibition fees and memberships fees must be listed separately. *Art supplies* – purchased art supplies may be lumped together, but *books* should be kept separate.

There are other tax considerations your accountant will be able to tell you about; leasing a car might be advantageous for you. There are times when you may want to defer a client's payment of a bill. *Income averaging* is a way to help your tax situation when your income bounces up and down. Talk over such matters with your accountant.

Banking Your Business

You need all the financial information you can get when starting a business. Make an appointment with your bank. Sit down and tell them what you are doing – setting yourself up in business as an artist. Be frank about how much, or how little, money you have. You may be surprised at how helpful a bank can be. If it disappoints you, try another bank. They can tell you exactly how to set up your savings accounts, checking accounts, and retirement plans to your best advantage. They will probably give you a work sheet to figure out your assets, and tell you the kinds of loans for which you qualify. It is well worth a morning's time. Business is business and art is art – but the two must meet.

Barter

Don't be afraid to live by your talent in any honest way. Barter is a way that you might make up to three-fourths of your income. In a shaky economy, it may be more likely a way to get you what you need than other means.

Ghost of Freedom, 48x40 inches, acrylic on masonite, by Edna Wagner Piersol.

This is the cowboy who almost turned into a Volkswagen when a young man offered his car in exchange for the painting. I didn't need an extra car at the time, and barter only works well when you trade for things you are ready to buy.

Living space is one thing that you might obtain this way. Once, while completing a project, I toyed with the idea of advertising in the *Wall Street Journal* for living space in exchange for artwork of any kind. I didn't have to go that far. An acquaintance put a house at my disposal in exchange for artwork. It's odd that as soon as that happened, I began to feel as though I was taking advantage of my friends. That was silly. I've come to realize that people do not offer things unless they want to do so. Artists are special to many people; being able to be a part of an artist's creativity is an honor to them. It's a genuine feeling.

Sometimes you can suggest the barter and other times your clients will suggest it. It can come as a delightful surprise. My large painting of a cowboy titled, "Ghost of Freedom" had been on exhibit in a restaurant for a week, when I received an urgent call from a young man who wanted to trade his Volkswagen for the painting. I didn't need an extra car, so he lost out. Another time, when I needed caps on my teeth, my dentist was amenable to a trade. Be careful when you do this. Try to avoid deals that could have disastrous results. You don't have much recourse when you're having teeth fixed. It worked out well for me and probably will for you too, but give it due thought before you act.

Barter opportunites are everywhere. Do you need body work done on your car? Maybe the owner of the shop would like a good painting of his business place to use in advertising. Better yet, he might like a painting of his favorite car. Do you need display space for your paintings? Try approaching the owner of a boutique with the offer of doing her portrait for the space you'd like. Once I traded sailing lessons for drawing lessons. Do you need typing or editing done? Try trading. Is there a grocery store owner in your area who has several children and would like portraits in exchange for groceries? If you arrange a few barter agreements before you set out to support yourself by artwork, you can gain a little sense of security.

There are barter groups in many parts of the country these days that specialize in getting together people who want to barter. They take a small fee or commission. There is little that you need that you can't get by bartering if you look hard enough.

Remember, barter is income. You must report it to the Internal Revenue Service. You have to set a fair, proveable value on what you are trading, as does the person with whom you are trading. There must be written proof of the value of the item. (Contact the IRS for more details.)

When bartering, be sure to get a written agreement. It may not be necessary for little things or quick one-time exchanges, but if going into something like a living arrangement, it is best to get a lease.

You have probably guessed that barter works much better with small business owners and individuals than large corporations. It would be silly to try to trade a portrait for a share of ITT – but who knows?

Chapter Ten

Can Marriage Survive an Artist?

Artists are like everyone else. Some live alone and like it; some live alone and *don't* like it. Some live together as man and wife, or whatever, and like it; some live together and *don't* like that. It seems self-evident that none of us can help but be deeply affected by those who live with or near us. Does this condition affect artists more than others? Based on my own experience, it seems this might be true. In discussing the problem with a variety of people, both artists and nonartists, I was amazed at the interest the subject evoked. There is an issue here that deserves more exploration.

On the premise this subject should be discussed, I screened the results of many conversations and came up with the following insights into what makes or breaks a marriage of creative people. As a fellow artist, I thought you might be interested in what others feel on this subject, one that has an impact on each of us one way or another.

Judy Wiesman
Artist married to musician
Atlanta, Georgia

Q. Both you and your husband, Bob, have active, creative careers. What do you think has made your "artistic" marriage work?

A. After sixteen years of marriage, we feel that not only can a marriage survive an artist or two, but is, if anything, easier for us because one of the major causes of divorce has been eliminated – boredom, being in a rut. We have a mixed marriage: performing and visual arts. Therefore, we do not compete with each other. While Bob has his undergraduate degree in design, his life is music. On the other hand, I have a strong music background in piano and violin, but would rather "paint than pick." Early in our marriage we did have some problems. I wanted Bob to paint more. He is capable of excellent work. Bob wanted me to "learn fiddle" and perform with him. We soon came to realize that we both were happier pursuing our own interests while supporting each other's.

Bob is the chief and best critic of my completed work, as well as my organizer and marketing planner. I am continually amazed at his ability to do all this, plus his ability to perform, to play literally any instrument with strings. I still, always, enjoy his performances. Bob gets the worst of the deal. There are a lot more paintings to pack, load and unload when I'm doing a show, than [there are] instruments and sound equipment when he is doing a performance.

With the addition of a family, our situation expanded. We always knew that any children of ours would either love or hate art and music, but would never be indifferent to them. Since the age of two, the girls have been performing with their Dad and now, at the ages of ten and twelve, are seasoned entertainers with "The Wiesman Family Singers." Recently, there has been a change in the family act. Formerly, Bob would completely plan the show – songs, arrangements, everything. Now, the planning has a three-person input with the girls also announcing what numbers they wish to perform, who will sing the lead, and who will play what instrument. In this part, I enjoy remaining in the background and find it hard to keep a straight face at times.

Art-wise, the girls are always painting or involved in a craft. I suppose the best is still to come. In the near future, we are doing a local show where I am exhibiting, Bob and the girls are performing, and the girls are also participating in the art realm. Cheri will be doing face painting, while Teri is doing a series of small monster paintings for sale.

As might be gathered, with all our interests, we seem to be continually on the go. Sometimes we wonder when we will actually have a night at home, with nothing planned, to just relax. But do we really want that? Even long trips are easy with everyone singing and playing instruments on the road.

In summation, I suppose that our life-style might not be everyone's "cup of tea," but we wouldn't have it any other way. All artists are a

Critters, 26x30 inches, acrylic, by Judy Wiesman.

little bit crazy, but we truly love what we are doing. I'm afraid that both Bob and I would be frustrated and bored to tears if we were confined in a routine family environment and nine-to-five jobs.

What's really nice is that with artist friends, Bob is Judy's husband; while with musicians, I am Bob's wife. Perhaps it is this give-and-take that makes having two or more artists in a family a lot of fun – even after sixteen years.

Female artist
Married twenty-six years
to a nonartist
Now divorced

Q. What do you think about artists and marriage? Or relationships?
A. I'd like a chance, again, to make one work. I think I could be much better at it now than I was at twenty-three. I tried, but we never saw eye to eye. I suppose he thinks he tried, too.

I remember telling him, before we were married, never to treat art as a rival, because I was afraid he'd lose. He promised he wouldn't and then began to try to compete with my career as soon as the marriage vows were over. The minute he knew my mind was totally on painting, he would need a button sewn on his shirt, even though he had five other shirts he could have worn at that moment. I also suspect he could have used a needle [and thread]. He seemed capable at things he wanted to do.
Q. Would it have worked better if you had been married to an artist?
A. I don't know, but I think that now I'd understand an artist, writer, or musician better than a nonartist. I'd like that kind of relationship now, but don't think I could have handled it when I was younger – another ego to contend with.
Q. Does a woman artist really need a husband?
A. Everyone needs someone. We aren't meant to be solitary creatures, at least I'm not. But as we get older, it becomes harder to adjust our life to another's. Art is all-consuming, 90 percent of the time, yet it's not enough sometimes.
Q. What kind of man would you like in your life?
A. Someone who stimulates my mind. Someone who understands the moods of an artist and takes the time to find out how to respond.

I'd expect to do that for him, too; to find out what he needs and try to provide that. If two people were working together like that, how could they lose?

Male artist
Married twenty years
Now divorced

Q. What do you think about marriage between two artists?

A. I think a marriage or a relationship could survive, but the two artists involved must be flexible. They are two very special people. There are two egos to serve, both already spoken for, both already married to art.

Q. Can you pinpoint anything that happened in your marriage that illustrates this?

A. It was a matter of priorities. We didn't agree often. For instance, she wanted to clean up the place all the time and cleaning doesn't always go with my work. I think we used this kind of thing against one another.

Q. Maybe as an excuse for the real underlying problem?

A. Yes. The first commitment must be to one's own needs and each must realize this. When you are young, though, it is the wrong time to *think*. Reason should balance emotion if *possible*, but it doesn't always.

Female artist
Married twenty-eight years
to a military man

Q. How did you adjust to marriage to a nonartist?

A. I was an art major, not finished with schooling, when we married. After marriage there was a typical husband-wife relationship. We had a family and a fairly structured home life. My art career was submerged – that was not unusual for those times. My husband was not supportive of my art career. Then he went away on military duty for one year and the worm turned. When he came home, I had received peer approval and his opinion of my art no longer mattered to me.

Q. How are you getting along now?

A. We function in two different worlds.

Q. Is that good? Is the marriage going to survive?

A. If it does, it will be because I decide there is no better situation for me. An artist isn't structured. His desire for that can't help but cause conflicts. I have had to comply by creating only from nine to five. I bargained to be wife, social secretary, mother. Then I changed. He didn't. Artists always evolve; [they] can't help it. I was not a jelled professional when I married and artists never stop evolving. In my case, my husband evolved, too – to one of the best in his field – but he has no interest in what I'm doing. I feel I am interested in his work and admire what he is doing.

Q. How could this be resolved?

A. I've resolved it by recognizing he won't change; discussing it – very important – which helps me (he's trying, but not changing); and seeking approval among my fellow artists and keeping the most important part of my life separate from my marriage.

Q. What are your reasons for keeping the marriage?

A. Twenty-eight years is a lot of common experience. Four beautiful children. I have a great deal of respect for, and I care enough for this man, to want to continue. The end of the story will come when my husband retires. If he makes me choose between sitting at home, rocking and holding his hand, and my career – he'll lose.

Q. Did his military travel affect your career?

A. Yes, but it wasn't all bad. We lived so many places that I had to constantly re-establish my career. That kept me competing and fighting, never complacent. That's good.

Male artist
Married thirty years
to a nonartist

Q. What has you wife contributed to your career?

A. Everything. And I do mean everything. She has, in a sense, given up her own creative life to support mine.

Q. Is that good?

A. I think it has contributed to making our marriage work. I won't say that it wouldn't have worked anyway. She has enough art background that I think she might have been able to become an artist, but chose not to. She chose to be an artist through me.

Q. Did you ask her to give up her life to yours?

A. No. I don't think I did, but I know she felt I wanted it that way. It has worked well. She is my agent and my best publicist. She also guards my time so that I can paint and produce. There are times, though, when I feel almost too much gratitude. It overshadows other feelings for her. Then I have to come back to the real reason we are together.

Q. Do you want to say more about that? I sense that you are getting on very intimate ground.

A. I'll say more. She has been very understanding of all my moods or we would not have made it. There have been times when I felt things for other women, felt they were more exciting than my wife, wished she would be more independent. I've had students and colleagues who stimulated my mind in a way that she did not always have time for, while raising my children and overseeing my career. I have sometimes wanted to just see what it would be like to live in a different way, but being a moral man, I never did. She tolerated my friendships with other women. I think she always knew they were only friendships, but I'm not sure I always did. The wife of a male artist who gets involved in workshops and shows has a lot to think about when her husband is away. I wonder if I'd have handled it as well if the shoe had been on the other foot.

Q. What do you mean?

A. Well, I've had some women artist friends who had the same problem with their husbands. They wanted more creative give-and-take, more time to smell the roses with another "kindred soul," which their husbands were not. I'm afraid I always identified with the guys—the husbands. I think I wanted freedom for myself that I was not willing to give to my wife. But I never took that freedom. And I'm sure I would not be the artist I am without her constant support.

Barbara Gresham
Artist
Louisville, Kentucky

Q. You have lived and worked in Pennsylvania, Kentucky, Georgia – wherever your husband's life has taken you. How do you manage being wife, mother, and artist?

A. From the very beginning, the dual roles of homemaker and artist have spawned strange combinations of humor and drama, of tension and smiles. I see the roles as two true parallel lines, one occasionally soaring on ahead of the other. The success of their coexistence depends solely on the bridges built from one to another. Bridges have to be built from both sides and traversed from both sides. The temptation for an artist is to allow her/himself to become totally engulfed by the creative experience. While that is a welcome state of being during the process of the work itself, it can become a problem when there are relationships to be maintained with those who see themselves as "outsiders." Therein is the key perception. It is the manner with which husbands and wives see themselves that is crucial.

It is easy to understand why the spouse of an artist may feel an isolated mate, because part of this being engulfed by the creative experience is a very private thing. However, so much of the experience is made richer by the sharing of it, by the building of bridges. Basic to this sharing is the simple desire to communicate. The creative effort involves a searching of the soul, a constant confrontation with success and failure, and an openness to new ideas. These are entities which are very personal in nature, and the sharing of them requires an openness which leaves one quite vulnerable. It is much easier to share the particulars of an office job, a business decision, a plant operation, or even decisions involving the comings and goings of children, than to open up one's soul, and let someone else in on the painful drama and the rare elation of the creative search.

It is, perhaps, just as difficult to be on the receiving end. When a fellow human being lays open his innermost struggles, most people are quite uneasy, are repelled by the intensity of the communication. The spouse of an artist has to face this intensity with regularity. There are times when the creative search brings an agony of silence more difficult to bridge than the spoken frustration. Besides the frustrations within the work itself, artists face constant criticism from media critics and amateur critics alike, constant fluctuations and fickleness on the part of museums, galleries, and the buying public. In short, it is an explosive, unsteady affair. Perhaps some marriages just aren't up to the added strain.

With an attitude of dedication, however, these seemingly negative facets of an artist's life could be turned into positive opportunities to enrich and deepen all communication between artist and mate. It is much more difficult for the marriage to get by on shallow commitments, and perhaps that is really a good thing. The world through the artist's eye is full of surprises, unique juxtapositions, and often a mysterious sense of déjà vu. A marriage that determines itself sound enough to share those things has depth and the elasticity for change. It truly is not a threat; it is an opportunity for a deeper, more whole marriage. If the crucial bridges of trust and sharing are established on this profound level, the bridges of a more particular nature seem to span themselves. If there are children involved, there is the usual sharing of responsibility that goes along with both marriage partners working. The difference is the erratic schedule of an artist and the depth of involvement. As an artist-mother I can only present that particular role with the negatives and positives that pertain to it. Most are positives, thank goodness!

Q. How about your children – what do they think of your life?

A. I once heard of an interview with a famous musician in which he was asked if he minded the "unusualness" of his upbringing. When he was a child his mother spent four hours a day practicing the cello while he played quietly at her feet. For all he knew, all mothers did that! My children may not choose to be artists, but since my first child was two years old, I have spent four or more hours a day painting. So, that is "normal" to my children. What is a real bonus is that the creative experience, the seeking and finding of one's own answers,

Earth Cellar, 22x22 inches, watercolor, by Barbara Gresham.

the looking at the world visually and conceptually in a unique way, is also normal to them. The struggle of success and failure and the courage to be alone is right there in their own house, and I cannot help but believe that they will be stronger, yet more sensitive, human beings because of it.

The bridge that I build from the "artist's line" to the "others' line" must be one that invites my children to cross. Although much of my work I must do alone, many times I've invited them to paint with me or to go sit together in the woods to "see what we can see."

My children are no strangers to art exhibits, be it outdoor fairs or museums; that's another little bonus. Viewing exhibits in which there is one of Mom's paintings has become "old hat." So has viewing exhibits from which Mom's paintings have been rejected! The whole family shares the successes and the failures. Sometimes with extreme effort I have to lay aside the defeats and the victories (for either will dictate a narrow pathway) and continue the search from my own viewpoint. This is a particular dilemma which forces the visual artist to embrace the whole of life almost daily. To invite children into this world, in a way, forces them to embrace the whole of life, too. To keep the experience from becoming too overpowering, there must remain in the forefront the simple truth that personal victories and defeats are rather meaningless unless they are shared. As one artist friend reminded me, "Remember, art comes from life. Life does not come from art." Build your bridges.

Q. Your approach to life is great and I'm sure your children love it, but how do you and your husband keep your equilibrium?

A. The balancing act of artist-homemaker is rather like the old jokes about "the good news and the bad news." The good news is that it isn't a nine-to-five job, so I can be home when my children get off the school bus, I can plan corresponding vacation time with my husband, and, of course, I save so much gasoline, etc., not driving to work because I can work at home. The bad news is that it's difficult to explain to some others that it is still a job, that one must work regularly and in depth. It is also difficult to find true friends who will accept one's dedication to one's work without considering it a personal affront. Maybe that is why so many "arty types" stick together! The balancing act continues with volunteer work one is expected to do, because, after all, it isn't as if painting is a job – legitimate, that is. Also, the bad news is that if I hear, What a nice hobby at one more party, I might scream!

The good news is, it is all worth it. It is an approach to life which demands that I constantly examine my soul and the soul of life itself. It is a way of life which says that I will never feel like the lyrics of the song that Peggy Lee sings, "Is that all there is?" It is a way of living that has taught me that I will change in the way I see things, the way I react to things. I don't expect to stay the same. Therefore, I can accept more readily change in my husband and my children. The *fear* of change for us all is lessened.

There are a few frivolous things with which we have built bridges. My husband was once a dye chemist and the differences in the color vocabulary of a chemist and an artist proved rather amusing. I have a deep appreciation for working neutral colors; to him they are just "dirty." To him it is a red-brown; to me it is burnt sienna. The little dog I had for fifteen years carefully walked around all pieces of paper when I was painting (I paint on the floor), but went charging through and over anything when I wasn't. Even she was part of the bridge building.

One important observation about parallel lines is that, by definition, they never really converge. If two straight lines do cross each other, they must then go in different directions. Two parallel lines with bridges can go on into infinity.

Conclusion

In conclusion, I would like to share with you my philosophy of teaching painting and sharing ideas that has been with me throughout my professional life. *If you are going to become better at painting than I am – I might as well help you as much as I can and then take part in your glory.*

Farewell, happy painting and, most of all, happy living.

Index

Other North Light Books

Watercolor

Basic Watercolor Painting, by Judith Campbell-Reed. Step-by-step exercises to help artists develop their skills, with practical advice on presenting and pricing artwork. $14.95 paper; $21.95 cloth

Croney on Watercolor, by Charles Movalli. Using dozens of examples, Croney illustrates his five building blocks of art: drawing, composition, values, color, and technique. Exercises show how to develop the skills to paint with more artistic expression. $14.95 paper; $22.50 cloth

Painting Flowers with Watercolor, by Ethel Todd George. Full of technical instruction for capturing the character of flowers, including pointers on color, composition, and special effects in painting lilacs, peonies, and more. $19.95 cloth

Watercolor—The Creative Experience, by Barbara Nechis. Nechis encourages innovation and helps watercolorists expand technical skills and develop personal styles. She covers glazing, color, design, and gives sound advice on preparing artwork, keeping records, dealing with galleries. $14.95 paper

Watercolor Energies, by Frank Webb. Webb demonstrates his approach to painting and guides readers through the skills and thinking processes necessary for individual growth and artistic maturity. $14.95 paper; $22.50 cloth

Mixed Media

The Animal Art of Bob Kuhn, by Bob Kuhn. Basic procedures for sketching and creating pictures to reflect the natural habitat, with explanations on realism and animal character, motion, and attitudes shown in a portfolio of Kuhn's drawings and paintings. $15.95 paper

A Basic Course in Design, by Ray Prohaska. Covers the essential elements of design—form, composition, color—in easy stages leading artists into drawing and painting a picture, with discussions on monotype printing, creating and critiquing designs in acrylic, collage, impasto, and alla prima. $12.50 paper

The Basis of Successful Art: Concept and Composition, by Fritz Henning. Through discussions, illustrations, observations from well-known artists, Henning teaches specific "think stages" for formulating and developing ideas into complete works of art. With critiques of works from the Old Masters to contemporary artists. $16.95 paper; $24.95 cloth

Drawing and Painting Buildings, by Reggie Stanton. Includes all the fundamentals of architectural rendering: how to render building components, using props, selecting media and styles of presentation for residential and commercial projects. With instruction on perspective, short cuts, composition, and rendering textures. $17.95 cloth

Encyclopaedia of Drawing, by Clive Ashwin. Nearly one hundred entries on the materials, history, and techniques of drawing with hundreds of illustrations. $22.50 cloth

The Painter's Guide to Lithography, by John Muench. Describes what the *painter* needs to know about creating lithographs, avoiding unnecessary technical jargon to encourage artists to try this process. $14.95 paper; $22.50 cloth

Painting Nature: Solving Landscape Problems, by Franklin Jones. How to paint landscapes in oil, watercolor, and acrylic demonstrated in detail, including the effects of weather, light, and color. $16.95 cloth

The Roller Art Book, by Sig Purwin. How the brayer, or small hand roller can be used by graphic artists, designers, painters—with dozens of demonstrations on how to apply this technique for innovative results. $11.95 paper

6 Artists Paint a Landscape, by Charles Daugherty. Each of the artists demonstrates his approach, method, and procedure for painting the same rural landscape and describes the challenges of planning and composing the picture. A unique opportunity to watch artists at work expressing their distinct interpretations of a subject. $14.95 paper

6 Artists Paint a Still Life, by Charles Daugherty. Each artist selects and portrays the same objects gathered from an old barn, describes the methods and materials chosen for the painting, and demonstrates step-by-step every composing, sketching, and painting stage in creating the still life. $14.95 paper

Oil Color/Art Appreciation

Controlled Painting, by Frank Covino. How to create realistic pictures in oil and acrylics in the classical manner: estimating values, selecting and mixing color, accurate drawing, creative composing, using the camera. $14.95 paper; $22.50 cloth

The Immortal Eight, by Bennard Perlman. A biographical look at the eight rebellious artists who formed the Ashcan School of Art led by Robert Henri and whose ideas influenced modern American art. $24.95 cloth

Commercial Art/Business of Art

The Art & Craft of Greeting Cards, by Susan Evarts. How to create personalized designs for greeting cards, announcements, and invitations, with advice on preparing artwork, applying techniques including monoprints, stencils, silk screen, type selection, color separation, and marketing the finished design. $13.95 paper

The Artist and the Real World, by Frederic Whitaker. Essays from a distinguished watercolorist on the politics of the art scene, the manipulation of art show juries, the role of critics and museum directors, and business practices that affect every artist's professional career. $14.95 cloth

Graphics Handbook, by Howard Munce. How to design and prepare art material for printing: the essentials of typography, copy fitting, paste-up, paper selection, and printing procedures for brochures, posters, greeting cards, booklets, and more. Filled with camera-ready art. $11.95 paper

To order directly from the publisher, include $1.50 postage and handling for one book, 50¢ for each additional book. Allow 30 days for delivery.

North Light Books
9933 Alliance Road, Cincinnati, Ohio 45242
Prices subject to change without notice.